WITHDRAWN

D1159707

free speech HANDBOOK

a practical framework for understanding our FREE SPEECH PROTECTIONS

Ian Rosenberg
art by Mike Cavallaro

Bridgeville Public Library
505 McMillen Street | Bridgeville, PA 15017
412-221-3737
Renew online @ www.bridgevillelibrary.org

:01
First Second

NEW YORK

First Second

Published by First Second
First Second is an imprint of Roaring Brook Press,
a division of Holtzbrinck Publishing Holdings Limited Partnership
120 Broadway, New York, NY 10271
firstsecondbooks.com

Text © 2021 by Ian Rosenberg
Illustrations © 2021 by Mike Cavallaro
All rights reserved

This book is a graphic novel adaptation of *The Fight for Free Speech: Ten Cases That Define Our First Amendment Freedoms*, which was published in 2021 by NYU Press.

Following graphic conventions common in comic books, some text in this book has been bolded to add emphasis. In quoted text, this emphasis may be attributed to the book's author and not to the original speaker.

Library of Congress Control Number: 2021903422

Our books may be purchased in bulk for promotional, educational, or business use. Please contact your local bookseller or the Macmillan Corporate and Premium Sales Department at (800) 221-7945 ext. 5442 or by email at MacmillanSpecialMarkets@macmillan.com.

FIRST
EDITION

First edition, 2021
Edited by Mark Siegel, MK Reed, and S. I. Rosenbaum
Cover design by Kirk Benshoff
Interior book design by Sunny Lee and Madeline Morales

Drawn on an iPad in Clip Studio Paint. Colored in Photoshop.

Printed in China

ISBN 978-1-250-61975-4
1 3 5 7 9 10 8 6 4 2

Don't miss your next favorite book from First Second!
For the latest updates go to firstsecondnewsletter.com and sign up for our enewsletter.

BY ART
WE LIVE

contents

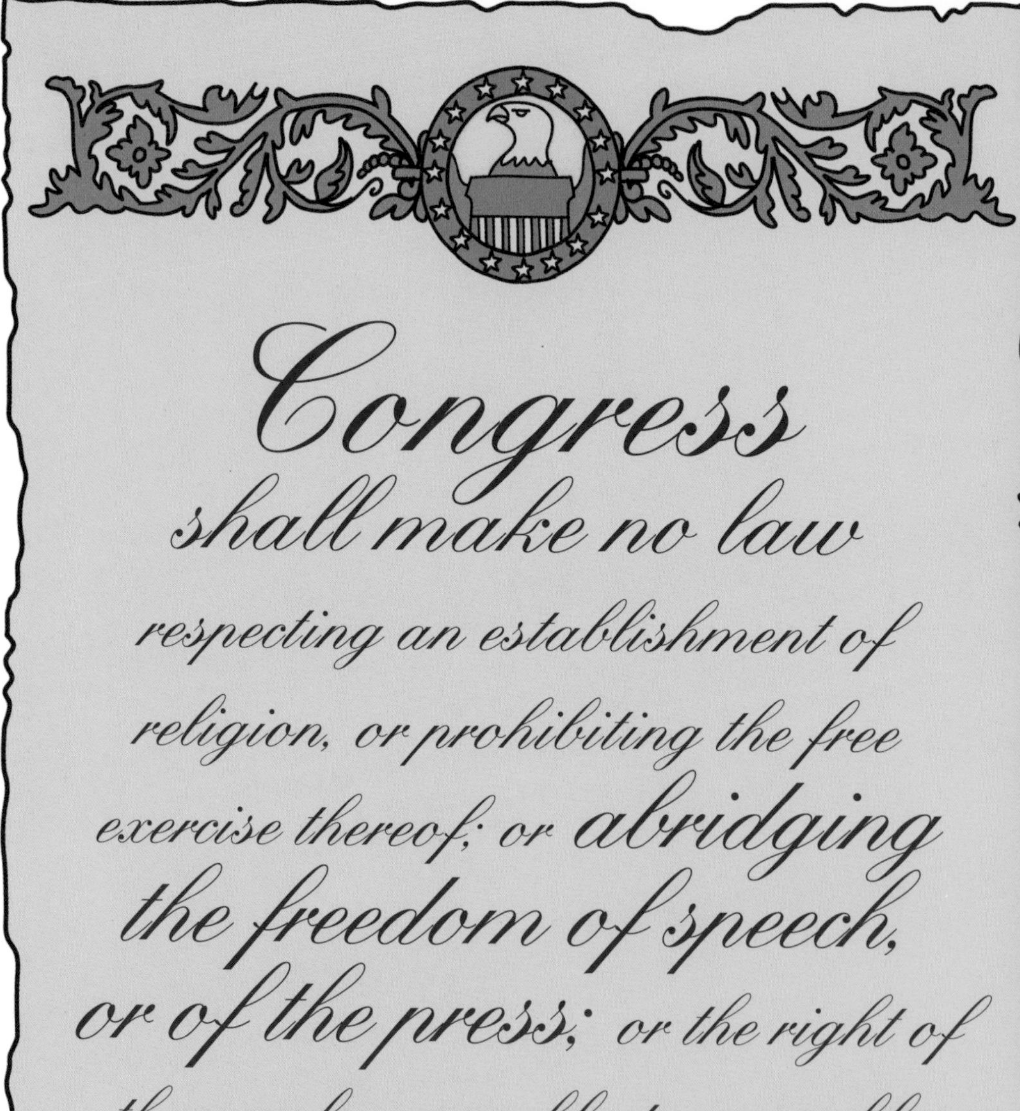

Congress

shall make no law

respecting an establishment of religion, or prohibiting the free exercise thereof; or **abridging the freedom of speech, or of the press;** or the right of the people peaceably to assemble, and to petition the Government for a redress of grievances.

For Alice and Leo

—IR

Introduction

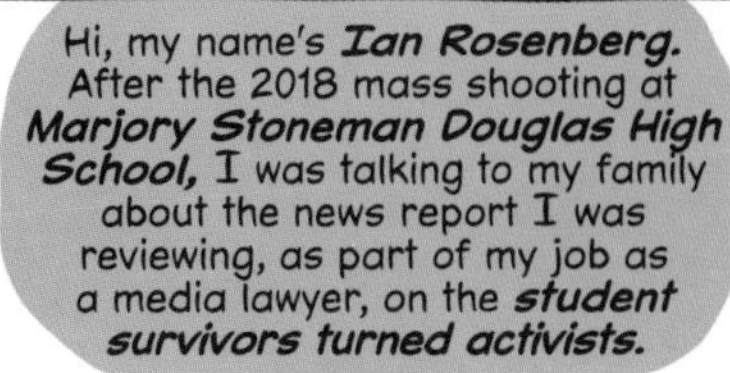

Hi, my name's Ian Rosenberg. After the 2018 mass shooting at Marjory Stoneman Douglas High School, I was talking to my family about the news report I was reviewing, as part of my job as a media lawyer, on the student survivors turned activists.
My children (at the time ages twelve and ten) became very serious about what would happen if they left school during the day to join the National School Walkout protests.
Could they be punished? What were their rights?

Americans of all ages are confronted with increasing frequency by a barrage of free speech questions. And while Americans are demanding free speech, they are often doing so without necessarily knowing what their rights really entail.

In our current cultural landscape, The Free Speech Handbook is a user's guide for combating ignorance and bringing an understanding of free speech law to all.

Come with me and travel through the past.
We will meet the unlikely pioneers who went before us, and let their journeys illuminate our free speech freedoms today.

Chapter 1:
THE WOMEN'S MARCH AND THE MARKETPLACE OF IDEAS

The Women's March of 2017.
What began as a post-election Facebook message transformed into more than 3 million women and men demonstrating across the globe at more than 300 sister events.
TELL ME WHAT DEMOCRACY LOOKS LIKE!
THIS IS WHAT DEMOCRACY LOOKS LIKE!
MY BODY MY
RISE UP
OUR RIGHTS ARE NOT UP FOR GRABS. NEITHER ARE WE.
OUR ARMS ARE TIRED FROM HOLDING THESE SIGNS SINCE THE 1920s
MY NANA DIDN'T FLEE RUSSIA FOR THIS!

Thank you for understanding that sometimes we must put our bodies where our beliefs are.
Gloria Steinem, feminist standard-bearer and honorary chairwoman of the event.

Coming the day after the inauguration of President Donald Trump, the March was also a protest of his election and offered a defiant rebuke of his nascent administration.

The next 1,459 days of the Trump administration will be 1,459 days of ***resistance.***
Angela Davis, civil rights activist.

Celebrities from the art and music worlds were front and center as featured speakers. Madonna caused controversy in some circles, as usual, because of her speech that day.

Yes, I'm *angry.* Yes, I am *outraged.* Yes, I have thought an awful lot about *blowing up the White House.*

But I know that this won't change anything. We cannot fall into despair. We must love one another or die. I choose ***LOVE.***

The Secret Service had ***no comment*** on her statement.

But others ***did.***

Madonna ought to be *arrested!*
FOX NEWS
NEWT GINGRICH
FORMER HOUSE SPEAKER

A hundred short years ago she most likely would have been not only ***arrested,*** but sentenced to years of ***jail time.***

Madonna, and ***all*** the marchers, owe their ***First Amendment protections*** to one tenacious young immigrant who set in motion the ***events*** that changed our relationship to ***free speech.***

In 1913 ***Mollie Steimer*** arrived at Ellis Island at the age of sixteen. Her family was fleeing Russia's virulent antisemitic discrimination and violence.

Standing just four foot, nine inches tall, she was later described by legendary anarchist and feminist ***Emma Goldman*** as "diminutive and quaint-looking...with an ***iron will*** and a ***tender heart.***"

She worked in a ladies' shirtwaist factory, laboring long hours to earn ***fifteen dollars a week*** to support herself and help her family.

Life was hard. Came home late, got up early. Things began to protest in me against a system of life where people who are hard workers have to struggle bitterly just to be able to exist.

Soon Steimer became deeply devoted to the ***anarchist*** ideals of ***collective action, communal property,*** and ***abolishing government.***

She joined up with a group of fellow Russian Jewish anarchists who met regularly at an apartment in ***East Harlem.***

Jacob Schwartz
Hyman Lachowsky
Jacob Abrams
Samuel Lipman

Together they published anarchist journals in Yiddish, first called *Der Shturm* ("The Storm") and later renamed *Frayhayt* ("Freedom").

In August of 1918, Steimer and her fellow anarchists were incensed by the news of a new mission launched as part of the United States' continuing involvement in ***World War I.***

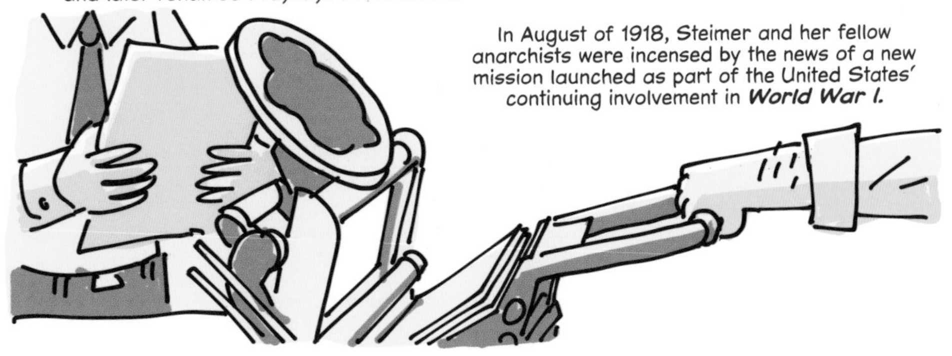

President ***Woodrow Wilson*** had just announced that he would be sending American troops to ***Russia.***

The decision was ***supposedly*** made to support ***Czechoslovak*** allies in the continuing fight against ***Germany.***
However, many viewed the action as an effort to help the ***"White" Russians*** and attack the ***"Red" Bolsheviks*** during their civil war.

Steimer saw it as an indefensible attempt to subvert the ***Russian Revolution.***

The group decided to produce two leaflets, one in ***English*** and one in ***Yiddish,*** furiously denouncing Wilson and his Russian endeavor. They printed 5,000 copies of each.

The English leaflet was titled

The Hypocrisy of the United States and Her Allies

It ***condemned*** Wilson and attacked his "shameful, cowardly silence about the intervention in Russia [that] reveals the ***hypocrisy*** of the plutocratic gang in Washington and vicinity."

The document goes on to lambaste the president as "too much of a ***coward*** to come out openly and say: 'We capitalistic nations cannot afford to have a ***proletarian republic*** in Russia.'"

It ends with a ***plea.*** "Will you allow the Russian Revolution to be ***crushed?***

"You: Yes, we mean ***YOU*** the people of America!...

"The Russian Revolution cries: 'WORKERS OF THE WORLD! AWAKE! ***RISE!*** PUT DOWN YOUR ENEMY AND MINE!'

"Yes friends, there is only one enemy of the workers of the world and that is CAPITALISM... ***AWAKE! AWAKE, YOU WORKERS OF THE WORLD!"***

It was signed simply: ***"Revolutionists."*** It also had a clarifying ***P.S.*** that adds:

"It is absurd to call us ***pro-German.*** We hate and despise German militarism more than do your hypocritical tyrants."

The second leaflet, in ***Yiddish***, titled ***"Workers Wake Up!!"*** addressed the same concerns, but in a more anguished tone and with a much more particular audience in mind.

ארבייטער וואכט אויף!!

Pointedly addressing "Workers in the ammunition factories," it announces that "you are producing ***bullets, bayonets, cannons,*** to murder not only the Germans, but also your dearest, best, who are in Russia and are ***fighting for freedom."***

In contrast to the **vaguer** advocacy of the English leaflet, this one made a specific call for **action:**
"**Workers,** our reply to the barbaric intervention has to be a **general strike!** An open challenge **only** will let the Government know that not only the **Russian Worker** fights for freedom, but also here in America lives **the spirit of Revolution.**

"Do not let the Government **scare** you with their wild punishment in **prisons, hanging and shooting.** We must not and will not betray the splendid fighters of Russia. **Workers, up to fight.** Woe unto those who will be in the way of progress. **Let solidarity live!"**
This one was signed, **"The Rebels."**

Steimer took most of the leaflets to scatter surreptitiously around the city. She threw some from Lower East Side rooftops and several people who found them were so **provoked** that they contacted **the police.**

Her **distribution** and these **words** were so shocking as to make New York City **headlines** the next day.
CITY EDITION
Seditious Circulars Scattered in Streets
THE NEW YORK NEWS
Wilson Attacked in Circulars from Roofs of East Side

On August 23, 1918, Steimer took ***another*** batch to the factory she worked at, and tossed several out the bathroom window.
Although they couldn't read the Yiddish words, workers went to the ***police,*** who conducted a floor-by-floor search of the building.
They found that an employee of the American Hat Company, ***Hyman Rosansky,*** had punched in earlier than usual that day.
Where's this ***Rosansky*** fella at?
Rosansky revealed that he was scheduled to pick up more leaflets from the group ***that evening*** on East 104th Street.

Staking out the rendezvous point from nearby doorways, the police ultimately *nabbed* Steimer and all the other group members *one by one.*
The *interrogations* at police headquarters ranged from *civil...*
...to *violent.*
Steimer claimed that Lachowsky, Lipman, and Schwartz were *severely beaten.*
By early the next morning, all of them *confessed* to their involvement, without implicating one another.
The defendants were charged with violating the *Sedition Act,* enacted just three months earlier, which made almost *all* speech *critical* of the government a *crime.*

Sedition Act
Specifically, they were accused of conspiring to "unlawfully utter, print, write and publish...disloyal, scurrilous and abusive language" about the U.S. government that was intended to bring it "into contempt, scorn, contumely and disrepute [and]... to incite, provoke and encourage resistance" to the war.

In addition to Steimer and her associates, more than 2,000 individuals would ultimately be prosecuted under the act, resulting in over 1,000 convictions.
The night before their trial, Jacob Schwartz died in the prison ward of Bellevue Hospital.
An autopsy determined that pneumonia was the cause of death, but his fellow defendants vehemently rejected that conclusion and believed police brutality was to blame.
During her trial testimony, the New York Tribune reported that Steimer clenched her fist and almost screamed:
I insist that Schwartz was killed by the police!
Farewell, comrades. When you appear before the court I will be with you no longer. Struggle without fear, fight bravely. I am sorry I have to leave you

On ***October 14,*** the anarchist speech trial began in federal district court in Manhattan. Unfortunately for the defendants, a visiting judge from Alabama named ***Henry DeLamar Clayton Jr.*** would be presiding.

Clayton was ***racist, anti-women's suffrage, anti-immigrant,*** and ***antisemitic.***

VOTE!

Clayton seemed ***unable*** or ***unconcerned*** about hiding his ***distaste*** for the ***immigrant defendants*** and their lawyer, ***Harry Weinberger,*** whose parents were Hungarian Jewish immigrants.

During ***Abrams's*** testimony, he ***twice*** asked,
Why don't you go back to ***Russia?***

At another point with Abrams on the stand, Clayton demonstrated his unwillingness to consider the defendants as Americans.
This government was built on a revolution...

When our forefathers of the American Revolution—
Your what?
My forefathers—

Do you mean to refer to the fathers of this nation as YOUR forefathers?

We are all a big human family.
Those that stand for the people, I call them father.
But the judge had made his point, and the jury had no doubt gotten it.

Clayton's ***condescending*** treatment of ***Steimer*** was no better, but she continued to ***rebelliously assert her beliefs.*** She refused to ***stand*** when the judge entered, and the bailiff called ***"all rise"*** to no avail.

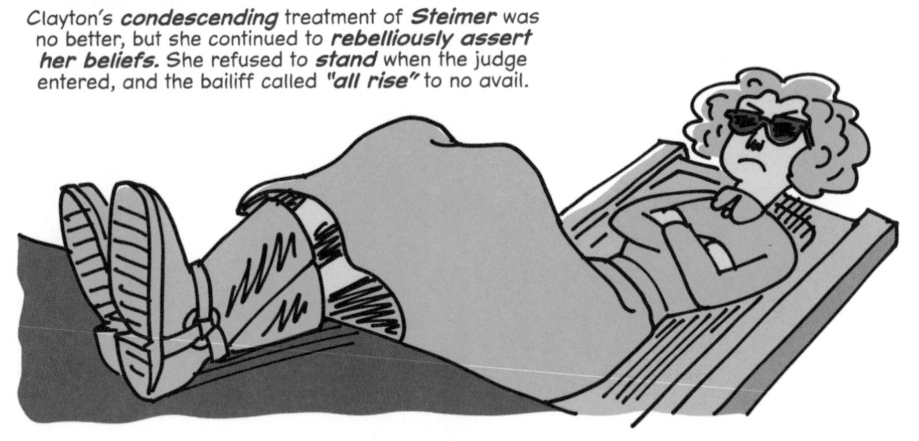

When questioned on whether she was ***an anarchist,*** Steimer pressed to define her philosophy in her own terms:

By anarchism, I understand a new social order, where no group of people shall be governed by another group of people.

Individual freedom shall prevail in the full sense of the word. Private ownership shall be abolished.

We shall not have to struggle for our daily existence, as we do now. No one shall live on the product of others.

Every person shall produce as much as he can and...receive according to his need.

Instead of striving to get money, we shall strive towards education, towards knowledge...

To the fulfillment of this idea I shall devote all my energy, and, if necessary, render my life for it.

Weinberger made a strenuous final effort to persuade the jury to support free speech in an epic two-hour closing argument.
He contended that the defendants were not supporting the German cause, and therefore were not encouraging resistance to the American war effort.
He maintained that even immigrant anarchists had...
...the right to question and protest against an army being sent to Russia, to fight the Bolsheviki.
They had the right, not because they are American citizens, because they are not, but because they are HERE and free speech is guaranteed to all citizens and noncitizens.
Despite Weinberger's valiant efforts, the outcome of the two-week trial was hardly in doubt.
After little more than an hour, the jury returned guilty verdicts for Abrams, Lachowsky, Lipman, Rosansky, and Steimer.

For the ***men,*** Clayton imposed the ***maximum sentence*** of ***twenty years each,*** and he gave Steimer ***fifteen.***
20
15
As Steimer responded to her sentence, Clayton attempted to ***cut her off.***
I'm not going to ***permit you*** to make a ***soap-box oration,*** Mollie—
NEVERTHELESS, SHE PERSISTED
Though you have ***sent troops*** to Russia, though you have sent soldiers to ***slaughter*** our ***revolutionists,*** you ***cannot crush*** our ***revolutionary spirit.***
The armistice bringing an ***end*** to World War I was only ***weeks away...***
...but Steimer and her anarchist comrades' ***constitutional battle for free speech*** had only begun.

A ***year*** had passed by the time the ***Supreme Court*** heard their case in ***October of 1919.*** Harry Weinberger summarized his brief in terms that described a sweeping question:
The point is put up... whether or not you have the ***right to criticize*** the President and the policies of the government.

He asserted that the ***freedom to speak*** out against the government had been protected by the framers of the Constitution, who viewed ***"the unabridgeable liberty of discussion as a natural right,"*** and therefore, he boldly claimed, the Sedition Act was ***unconstitutional.***

Weinberger also more pragmatically argued that there was ***insufficient evidence*** to support the verdict that the defendants had conspired to foster resistance to the war.

EVIDENCE

He reiterated the point that in calling for a ***munitions factory strike,*** the defendants were not supporting Germany, but rather seeking to ***defend Russia.***

He characterized the ***leaflets*** as merely "a public discussion of a public policy in reference to a country with which we were ***not*** at war."

Arguing on behalf of the government was ***Robert P. Stewart,*** who had been appointed earlier that year to be the first assistant attorney general in ***"charge of criminal matters"*** for the Department of Justice.

Stewart's main point was that the Court had ***upheld*** the constitutionality of the Espionage Act just seven months earlier, in a case called ***Schenck v. United States.***

ESPIONAGE ACT
OK!

Since the ***Sedition Act*** was an amendment to the ***Espionage Act*** and put similar limits on speech, he insisted that the ***Abrams*** convictions must be ***"equally constitutional."***

SEDITION ACT

In ***Schenck,*** during the war, two leaders of the ***Socialist party*** had been found guilty of ***obstructing the draft*** and causing ***insubordination in the armed forces*** in ***violation of the Espionage Act.***

Their actions had been to print and distribute 15,000 leaflets ***attacking the draft*** and urging ***peaceful resistance*** to it. Some of the leaflets were mailed directly to drafted men.

Justice Oliver Wendell Holmes Jr., writing for a ***unanimous*** Supreme Court, affirmed the convictions, including Schenck's ***ten-year sentence,*** in short order.

Holmes had served in the Union army during the ***Civil War*** and was an old-fashioned ***patriot*** who once said, ***"Damn a man who ain't for his country right or wrong."***

Justice Holmes expounded on why the specific limits on speech in the Espionage Act did **not** violate the First Amendment:
We **admit** that, in many places and in **ordinary times,** the defendants, in saying all that was said in the circular, **would** have been within their **constitutional rights.**
But the **character** of every act depends upon the **circumstances** in which it is done.
The most stringent protection of free speech would **not protect** a man in **falsely** shouting fire in a theatre and causing a **panic.**

With that fiery image, Holmes brought into the public consciousness what has been called "the most well-known—yet misquoted and misused—phrase in Supreme Court history."

It not only ***justified*** the wartime speech limitation for ***Schenck,*** but rhetorically spoke more ***broadly*** to the idea that limits on ***free speech*** should naturally be ***expected*** in our society.

Like a **zombie,** Holmes's metaphor continues to live on to our present day, **stalking** free speech wherever it goes, in the guise of **universally accepted wisdom.**
NOW PLAYING! "YOU CAN'T YELL FIRE..."

People who want to restrict free speech, invariably begin by saying some version of

"You can't yell fire..."

But limits on ***shouting fire*** are only ***justified*** if they are done ***falsely*** and end up ***causing a panic.*** No one would ever think of punishing someone for yelling ***"fire"*** when there was ***actually a fire burning.***

In fact, that person should be ***congratulated*** on potentially saving the lives of their fellow theatergoers!

In addition, if there is no ***panic*** or harm, then any speech restriction is ***unnecessary,*** and even ***worse,*** may ***deter*** people from calling out a warning when one is ***needed.***

Both of these often forgotten components—***falsity*** and ***harm***—are crucial to comprehending the ***true limits*** of the First Amendment and should be ***prerequisites*** in ***any*** consideration of prohibiting speech.

FALSITY
AND
HARM

If ***you,*** dear reader, take away ***nothing else*** from this book, please ***go forth*** and flaunt your knowledge of how to use this adage ***properly*** from now on.

So in ***Schenck,*** Holmes and the Court had decided that the First Amendment had ***no power*** to stop the government from ***imprisoning people*** for nonviolent speech that criticized the government.

HOLD MY BEER

Assistant Attorney General Stewart had every reason to believe that ***another unanimous judgment*** in the government's favor was sure to follow in ***Abrams.***

And yet, ***shockingly,*** Holmes himself was about to ***change course*** and lead the country on a new path toward a ***First Amendment revolution.***

Seven justices of the Court had no difficulty deciding that the defendants' convictions in ***Abrams*** should all be ***upheld.***

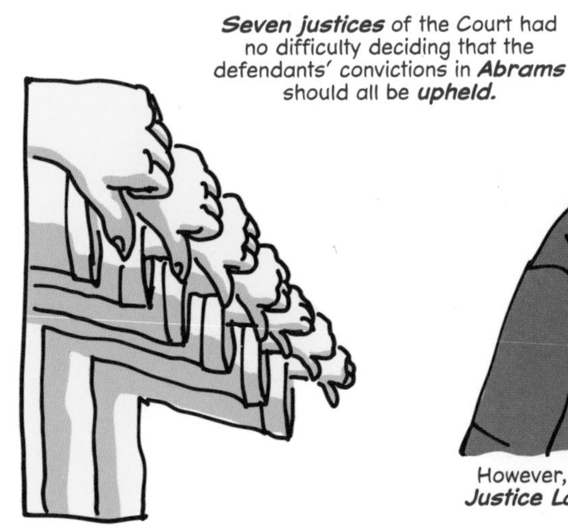

However, Justice Holmes, supported by his friend ***Justice Louis Brandeis,*** was thinking ***differently.***

As the majority opinion was being prepared, Holmes was about to write ***"twelve paragraphs that would change the history of free speech in America."***

What he wrote was so ***well reasoned*** and ***subversive...***

...that when he sent it around to his fellow justices for their consideration, it prompted a ***remarkable visit.***

A week later, ***three justices*** of the Supreme Court arrived unannounced at Holmes's town house.

They were there to personally ***appeal*** to Holmes to ***reconsider his position,*** and join them in supporting the convictions of the anarchists and the ***validity*** of the Sedition Act.

But their visit was to ***no avail.***

Three days later, the Supreme Court's decision in **Abrams v. United States** was announced. **Justice John Clarke** wrote the opinion for the seven-member majority, affirming the convictions.

Clarke **dismissed** what he described as the "faintly" argued First Amendment issues in a single sentence, holding that such claims had already been rejected in **Schenck.**
SCHENCK

After Clarke's summary of the case, Justice Holmes read his **dissenting opinion** from the bench to publicly emphasize how **"grievously misguided"** the majority opinion was, in his view.

It is only the **present danger** of **immediate evil** or an intent to **bring it about** that warrants Congress in setting a limit to the expression of opinion...
Nobody can suppose that the surreptitious publishing of a **silly leaflet** by an unknown man, without more, would present **any** immediate danger that its opinions would hinder the success of the government arms...
In this case, sentences of **twenty years'** imprisonment have been imposed for the publishing of two leaflets that I believe the defendants had **as much right to publish** as the Government has to publish the Constitution of the United States now **vainly invoked** by them.
The most **nominal punishment** seems to me all that possibly could be inflicted, unless the defendants are to be made to **suffer** not for what the indictment alleges, but for the **creed that they avow...**

20

Holmes constructed an expansive edifice for reconsidering the ***meaning*** of the First Amendment. He sought to convey ***why*** speech is ***dangerous,*** what free speech can do for society, and how ***strenuously*** we must resist the impulse to punish even the speech we hate. The result is the ***single most important paragraph*** in all of First Amendment law:
Persecution for the ***expression of opinions*** seems to me perfectly ***logical.*** If you have no doubt of your ***premises*** or your ***power,*** and want a certain result with ***all your heart,*** you naturally express your wishes in law, and ***sweep away all opposition.***
To allow ***opposition by speech*** seems to indicate that you think the speech ***impotent,*** as when a man says that he has squared the circle, or that you do not ***care*** wholeheartedly for the result, or that you ***doubt*** either your power or your premises.

But when men have realized that ***time*** has upset ***many fighting faiths,*** they may come to believe even more than they believe the very foundations of their own conduct that the ultimate good desired is better reached by ***free trade in ideas—that the best test of truth is the power of the thought to get itself accepted in the competition of the market...***

That, at any rate, is the theory of our Constitution. It is an experiment, as all life is an experiment.
Every year, if not every day, we have to wager our salvation upon some prophecy based upon imperfect knowledge.
The Constitution
While that experiment is part of our system, I think that we should be eternally vigilant against attempts to check the expression of opinions that we loathe and believe to be fraught with death...
...unless they so imminently threaten immediate interference with the lawful and pressing purposes of the law that an immediate check is required to save the country.
BAD IDEA
Only the emergency that makes it immediately dangerous to leave the correction of evil counsels to time warrants making any exception to the sweeping command, "Congress shall make no law...abridging the freedom of speech."
BAD IDEA

The **impact** of these words over time is hard to overstate. It would become **"the most quoted paragraph ever written about the freedom of speech."**
This **new vision** of the First Amendment eloquently articulated why the government should be **constitutionally prohibited** from punishing Americans for their speech, simply because the government opposed or **feared the ideas** in that speech.

It also placed **dissenting voices** at the **center,** not the **margins,** of First Amendment protection, even during wartime.

As noted dissenter **Justice Ruth Bader Ginsburg** had described, one of the primary purposes of a dissent is for **"appealing to the intelligence of a future day."**

Holmes's words measure up to that rare distinction: They not only **spoke** to the future, **they transformed it.**

THEORIES
BIG THOUGHTS
Central to this new free speech perspective was the metaphor Holmes conjured up that became known as the "marketplace of ideas."
BELIEFS
FACTS
Holmes turns to the ***marketplace*** to convey the ***value*** of searching for truth in a forum where the government ***cannot exclude*** critical voices from the public debate.
CONCEPTS 'R' US
FICTION
We should not, however, fail to recognize the substantial body of ***academic critique*** that has challenged the ***marketplace of ideas*** theory.
Much of this discussion centers around the question of ***who is truly heard in the marketplace?***
IDEAS IDEAS IDEAS
If ***women, minorities,*** and ***the poor*** are not granted ***equal opportunity*** to enter the market, how can their voices participate in the competition for ***truth?***

We must eschew abstractions of first amendment theory that proceed without attention to the dysfunction in the marketplace of ideas created by racism and unequal access to that market.

University of Hawaii at Manoa Professor of Law Emeritus ***Charles R. Lawrence III***

Think about whether the speech of the ***Nazis*** has historically enhanced the speech of the ***Jews.***

Has the speech of the ***Klan expanded*** the speech of ***Blacks?*** Has the so-called speech of ***pornographers*** enlarged the speech of ***women?***

In this ***context,*** apply to what they call ***the marketplace of ideas*** the question...Is there a ***relationship*** between ***our poverty*** in speech and ***their wealth?***

Feminist legal pioneer ***Professor Catharine A. MacKinnon***

The free market may be an effective ***economic system,*** but how does a mechanism designed to enable ***selling*** act as a model to facilitate ***truth seeking?***

SUGAR FROSTED
TRUTH FLAKES
TRUTH FLAKES

The influence of ***money and advertising*** dollars in a market-based system also raises real concerns about ***truth*** resulting from a process in which ***wealth*** buys you a ***bigger and better megaphone.***

Mark Twain is credited with saying that "a lie can travel around the world and back while the truth is still lacing up its boots." And that perception is ***supercharged*** in today's social media–paced world, in which the truth can be ***swamped*** under a ***tweet storm*** of instant ***falsehoods.***

There are those who would argue that whatever ***value*** the marketplace metaphor had ***in the past,*** it is becoming quickly ***outmoded*** in our internet age.

All of these powerful critiques justify ongoing debate. Grappling with the marketplace of ideas is vital for both those who seek to support our country's current approach to free speech and for those who wish to change it.

Putting metaphor and theory ***aside,*** how did the ***Abrams*** dissent actually change the law regarding advocacy of illegal action, if ***at all?***

The ***short answer*** is that it ***didn't***—at least not for a ***long time.*** It was not until ***fifty years*** after ***Abrams,*** in a case called ***Brandenburg v. Ohio,*** that a version of the ***Holmes and Brandeis test*** suggested in their dissent fully ***evolved*** into its modern and lasting form.

The ***Brandenburg*** holding states that only speech advocating illegal conduct that was ***directed*** and ***likely*** to trigger ***imminent*** illegal action is ***not*** protected by the First Amendment, and therefore can be ***prohibited*** as incitement.

BRANDENBURG
v.
OHIO

This progression, from ***punishment*** of speech about criminal conduct, to robust ***protections*** for such speech, is ***directly attributable*** to Holmes's decision to change his mind in ***Abrams.***

The remarkable ***evolution*** of First Amendment rights from ***virtually nonexistent*** to possessing a ***superhero-like strength*** demonstrates our country's ***common law judicial system*** in action.

The ***"common law"*** means law that comes from ***judicial interpretation and decisions,*** rather than ***legislative statutes.*** Each decision builds on the ***next,*** with courts abiding by the past decisions (often called ***precedents***) of the courts above them in their system.

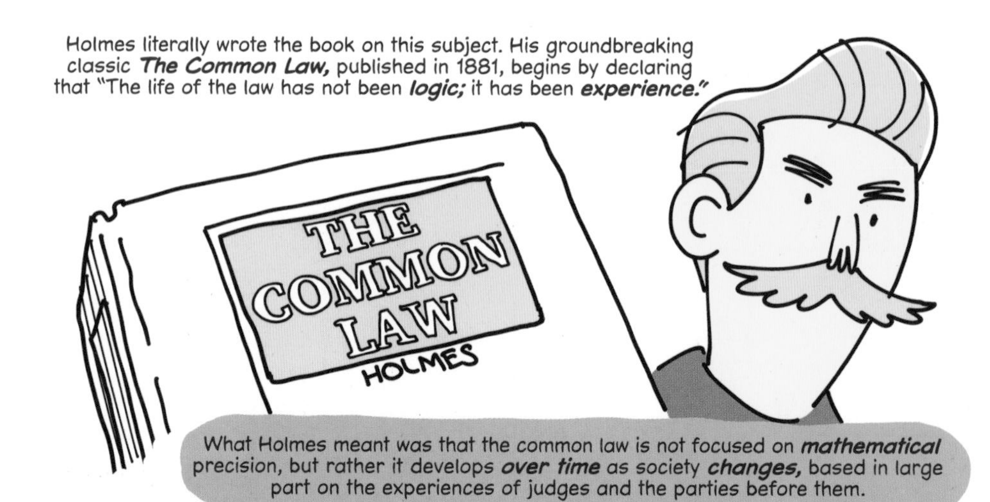
Holmes literally wrote the book on this subject. His groundbreaking classic ***The Common Law,*** published in 1881, begins by declaring that "The life of the law has not been ***logic;*** it has been ***experience.***"
THE COMMON LAW
HOLMES
What Holmes meant was that the common law is not focused on ***mathematical*** precision, but rather it develops ***over time*** as society ***changes,*** based in large part on the experiences of judges and the parties before them.

Whether you find this an ***inspiring process*** of ***messily evolving liberty*** or look with cynicism at its often ***lurching inconsistency,*** the ***Abrams*** case and its influence reflect the common law nature of our system for ***good and ill.*** And in doing so, it provides an origin story that is indispensable to understanding the First Amendment ***today.***

What did the ***Abrams*** decision mean ***at the time*** for the anarchists? It meant that by December of 1919, ***Abrams, Lipman, Lachowsky,*** and ***Steimer*** would all begin to serve their terms of ***fifteen to twenty years.***

They would remain incarcerated for the next ***two years,*** until the tireless lobbying efforts of ***Weinberger*** were able to get the new administration of ***President Warren Harding*** to commute their sentences on the condition that they be "at once ***deported*** to Russia, never to return."

Steimer initially ***refused*** to accept an amnesty deal.

I don't want to be ***deported.*** I don't want to be ***pardoned. You*** sentenced me; when all political prisoners will be freed, ***I*** will be freed.

But she later said she was ultimately prevailed upon to go along with the plan "when I was told that the boys are only waiting for ***me.***"

On November 23, 1921, Abrams, Lachowsky, Lipman, and Steimer were ready to depart to ***Russia*** from a pier in South Brooklyn aboard the ***SS Esthonia.***

Goodbye, all of you. I hope that America will be ***freer in the future*** than it is today.
From that time onward, their lives would be filled with even ***greater hardships.***

Persecuted and jailed in Russia for her anarchist beliefs, ***Steimer*** once again had no choice but to accept ***deportation.***

Lipman, who had become a Communist and a professor of economic geography, was ***killed*** as part of the Stalinist ***purges*** in the late 1930s.

And ***Lachowsky*** was most likely ***murdered*** in his native Minsk by the ***Nazis*** sometime after 1941.

Abrams and Steimer separately made their way to **Mexico** by 1942. Steimer would live there for the rest of her days, steadfastly committed to anarchist causes until her death in 1980.
We fought injustice in our humble way as **best we could;** and if the result was **prison, hard labour, deportations** and lots of **suffering,** well, this was something that every human being who fights for a **better** humanity has to expect.

Steimer would likely have felt ***right at home*** with the participants of ***the Women's March. Madonna's*** remark would not have shocked Steimer, although the lack of action taken against the speech might have ***surprised*** her.
RISE UP
OUR RIGHTS ARE NOT UP FOR GRABS. NEITHER ARE WE.
MY NANA DIDN'T FLEE RUSSIA FOR THIS!
LOV

The fact is that Madonna's statement would ***certainly*** be protected under the ***Brandenburg test,*** since it was neither "directed to inciting or producing imminent lawless action," from the crowd, nor "likely to incite or produce such action."

And ***Steimer*** deserves recognition for her role in making such speech ***protected*** under the First Amendment. On the day of her ***deportation,*** Mollie Steimer hoped America would be ***freer*** in the future. Her ***hope*** came to pass, and our speech is freer ***today*** than it ever would have been ***without*** her.

ESTHONIA

Chapter 2:
TAKE A KNEE AND THE PLEDGE OF ALLEGIANCE

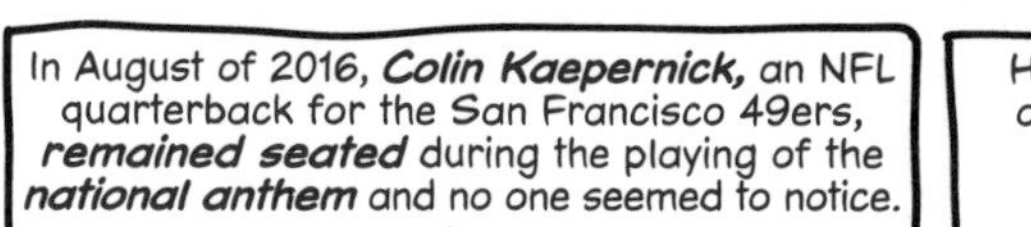
In August of 2016, ***Colin Kaepernick,*** an NFL quarterback for the San Francisco 49ers, ***remained seated*** during the playing of the ***national anthem*** and no one seemed to notice.

He did it ***again*** six days later and still no one commented. Perhaps it was because his throwing shoulder was sore and he wasn't in uniform.

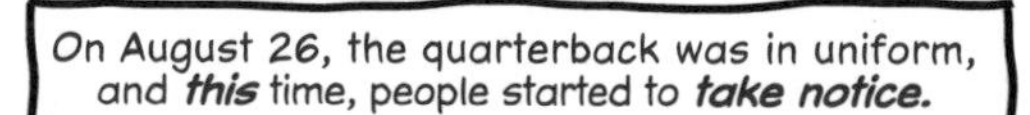
On August 26, the quarterback was in uniform, and ***this*** time, people started to ***take notice.***

I am not going to stand up to show ***pride in a flag*** for a country that ***oppresses Black people*** and ***people of color.***

To ***me,*** this is ***bigger*** than football and it would be ***selfish*** on my part to ***look the other way.*** There are ***bodies in the street*** and people getting ***paid leave*** and getting away with ***murder.***

Kaepernick did not notify the team about his protest.

This is not something that I am going to run by anybody. I am not looking for ***approval.*** I have to ***stand*** up for people that are ***oppressed.***
If they take football ***away,*** my ***endorsements*** from me, I know that I stood up for what is ***right.***

In response, the ***NFL*** issued a brief statement:

"Players are encouraged but not required to stand during the playing of the national anthem."

NFL

Two days later, Kaepernick spoke with the media and tried to provide ***greater context*** for his actions.
There is ***police brutality.*** People of color have been targeted by police.
So that's something that this country has to ***change.*** There's things we can do to hold them ***more accountable.***

Kaepernick was undoubtedly referring in part to the deaths just a month before of ***Alton Sterling*** and ***Philando Castile.***

Both men were ***Black,*** both ***killed by police*** within one day of each other, and both of their deaths had been captured on videos ***shared by millions,*** including Kaepernick.

This stand wasn't for ***me.***
This is because I'm seeing things happen to people that don't have ***a voice,*** people that don't have ***a platform*** to talk and have their ***voices heard,*** and ***effect change.***

What do you say to people who see the flag as a symbol for the military?
I have great respect for the men and women that have fought for this country. I have family, I have friends that have gone and fought for this country.

And they fight for freedom, they fight for the people, they fight for liberty and justice, for everyone.
That's not happening. People are dying in vain because this country isn't holding their end of the bargain up, as far as giving freedom and justice, liberty to everybody.
Nate Boyer, a former Army Green Beret and Seattle Seahawks long snapper, wrote an ***open letter*** addressed to Kaepernick for the *Army Times.*
"Even though my initial reaction to your protest was one of anger, I'm trying to listen to what you're saying and why you're doing it."
Kaepernick quickly reached out to Boyer and they met, along with 49ers safety ***Eric Reid.***

Our discussion led to the decision to not sit but to take a knee, to show respect to the people that felt hurt by that action.
Eric Reid
In the military, we take a knee all the time. It's the classic symbol of respect in front of a brother's grave site.
Nate Boyer
The next day, at their game against the San Diego Chargers...
O say can you see,
by the dawn's early light...
With little fanfare, the "Take a Knee" protests had begun and would develop into one of the most publicized and polarizing free speech controversies of the decade.
Seattle Seahawks cornerback Jerry Lane sat during the anthem, saying he was "standing behind Kaepernick."
Soccer star Megan Rapinoe said, "Being a gay American, I know what it means to look at the flag and not have it protect all of your liberties."
Denver Broncos linebacker Brandon Marshall took a knee and swiftly lost two sponsorship deals.
Four members of the Miami Dolphins took a knee.
Players on the Seahawks and Kansas City Chiefs linked arms with their teammates.
The entire WNBA Indiana Fever team took a knee together.

The protests were ***spreading.*** Kaepernick's ***individual stance*** was beginning to look like a ***movement.***

Michael Bennett of the Seattle Seahawks said the events in Charlottesville's deadly ***"Unite the Right"*** rally influenced his refusal to stand for the national anthem.
In his book, he divulged that he was also thinking about:
The gap between what we are taught the flag represents and the lived experience of too many people.
THINGS THAT MAKE WHITE PEOPLE UNCOMFORTABLE
MICHAEL BENNETT
and DAVE ZIRIN
By not standing, I wanted to honor the founding principles of this country—the freedom of self-expression, liberty, and the equal opportunity to pursue happiness—and challenge us to try to reach those goals.
I wanted to use my platform to inspire young people to see us not just as athletes or pitchmen for products, but as changemakers.
A month later, President Trump launched himself into the brewing culture war.
Wouldn't you ***love*** to see one of these NFL owners, when somebody ***disrespects our flag,*** to say, ***"Get that son of a bitch off the field right now, out, he's fired. He's fired!"***
USA!
USA!

NFL players were more ***unified*** than ever in their outrage over Trump's insulting profanity and message.

00
45
26

That weekend, more than 200 NFL players knelt or sat during the pregame national anthem.
However, the unity went only so far.

The vast majority of those actively protesting were Black. Like the military, sports was also supposed to be the place where race was secondary to the battle effort...
Howard Bryant
...and for years, sports had profited from the gauzy little lie that teammates battled together, understood each other, lived in such close proximity that maybe the rest of the country could learn from the game's brotherhood.
THE HERITAGE
BLACK ATHLETES, A DIVIDED AMERICA, AND THE POLITICS OF PATRIOTISM
HOWARD BRYANT
What Kaepernick revealed was that sports was no less divided along racial lines than the rest of the country, even if its workforce comprised a Black majority.

Meanwhile, Kaepernick had opted out of his contract with the 49ers, but as a free agent, no one would hire him.

NFL

In October, Kaepernick filed a grievance demanding an ***arbitration hearing*** on his claims that the ***owners*** were ***secretly acting together*** to keep him from playing.

"NFL and NFL Team Owners have colluded to deprive Mr. Kaepernick of employment rights in retaliation for Mr. Kaepernick's leadership and advocacy for equality and social justice and…in response to coercion and calculated coordination from the Executive Branch of the United States government."

In plain terms, Kaepernick claimed he was being ***excluded for his speech, by secret agreement.***

Principled and ***peaceful protest*** should ***not*** be punished and athletes should not be ***denied employment*** based on partisan political ***provocation*** by the Executive Branch of our government. Such a precedent threatens all patriotic Americans and harkens back to our ***darkest days*** as a nation.

Kaepernick's attorney ***Mark Geragos***

As Kaepernick's case progressed, the ***NFL*** moved toward trying to officially ***change*** its anthem policy.

OPERATIONS MANUAL
NFL
RU
BO

Standing on the field for the national anthem was not a standard practice for NFL players until 2009. The ***NFL rulebook*** did not mention the national anthem at all, and their ***game operations manual*** only stated that "all players must be on the sideline for the National Anthem…[and] ***should*** stand at attention."

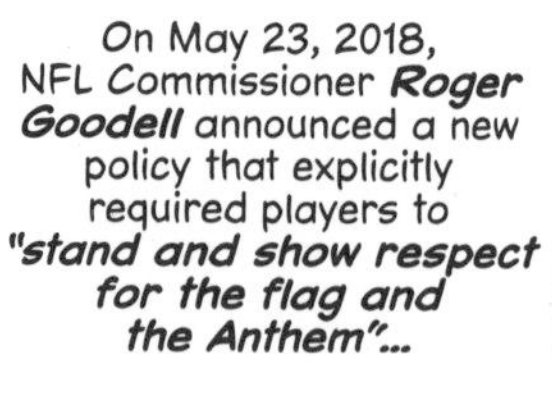
On May 23, 2018, NFL Commissioner ***Roger Goodell*** announced a new policy that explicitly required players to ***"stand and show respect for the flag and the Anthem"...***

...but allowed that those who "choose ***not*** to stand...may stay in the locker room or in a similar location ***off the field*** until after the Anthem has been performed."

The ***next day,*** President Trump praised the change on *Fox & Friends.*
You have to stand ***proudly*** for the national anthem, or you shouldn't ***be there.*** Maybe you shouldn't be in the country.
The NFL owners did the right thing.
EXCLUSIVE
FOX NEWS channel
TRUMP TALKS TO F&F ABOUT NEW ANTHEM POLICY
FOX & friends

Less than two months later, the NFL and the Players Association issued a joint statement that the policy was on hold, and it has remained indefinitely suspended.

TWEEEEE EEEET!!

The NFL owners' decision was an attempt to—

—thwart the players' constitutional rights to express themselves.
Malcolm Jenkins, Philadelphia Eagles

But was that policy ***actually*** a violation of NFL players' First Amendment rights?

A short, but incomplete, answer is no, because the First Amendment only applies to efforts by the ***government*** to restrict speech.

However, the public outcry on ***both sides*** of this controversy focuses less on what the NFL ***can*** do, and more on what the teams ***should*** do as a matter of free speech values.
Although the Supreme Court has never spoken on the national anthem ***specifically,*** it has ***twice*** considered whether public school students could refuse to ***pledge allegiance to the flag***—
—resulting in two strikingly ***different*** interpretations of our First Amendment rights.

In 1935, ten-year-old ***William Gobitas*** and his twelve-year-old sister ***Lillian*** lived with their family over their father's store, in the coal-mining town of Minersville, Pennsylvania.

Unlike 90% of their neighbors, who were Catholic, the Gobitas family were Jehovah's Witnesses.

The leader of their religion, ***Joseph Rutherford,*** had encouraged Witnesses to "object and refuse to salute the flag and pledge allegiance to it."

Witnesses ***respect*** the flag but going through rituals before an image or emblems was actually ***idolatry.*** Our relationship with Jehovah would strictly ***forbid*** this.
Lillian Gobitas, in a later interview

October 22, 1935.
I stopped saluting the flag! The teacher tried to put up my arm, but I held on to my pocket.
Miss Shofstal, I can't salute the flag anymore.
I respect your courage, Lillian.
I knew this was the moment. I did a lot of reading and checking in the Bible and I really took my own stand.
I didn't know whether it was right to stand up or sit down. So I sat down and the whole room was aghast.
After that, when I'd come to school they would throw a hail of pebbles and yell things like, Here comes Jehovah! They were just jeering at me.
For two weeks, the siblings refused to stand. Their school district superintendent, Charles E. Roudabush, was furious.
He sought to punish the children, but had been informed by the state's attorney general that a formal school flag-salute rule was required before he could take any disciplinary action.

At a school board meeting **Walter Gobitas** spoke on his children's behalf.
William and **Lillian** did not attend, but submitted handwritten letters to spell out their **beliefs.**
I do not salute the
flag not because I do not love
my country but I love my
country and I love God more
and I must obey His comm-
andments.
Your Pupil,
Billy Gobitas
Their heartfelt pleas were met with a cold shoulder.

The board ***unanimously approved*** a requirement that—

"All teachers and pupils [must] salute the flag of our country as a part of the daily exercises."

Roudabush immediately announced that William and Lillian were now officially ***expelled.***

As their ***demoralized*** father exited the meeting he cried out,
I'm going to take you to ***court*** for this!

With the support of the Jehovah's Witnesses' national legal counsel, Gobitas brought a lawsuit against the school district in the federal ***District Court in Philadelphia.***
More than a ***year*** had passed since the school board meeting, and in that time at least ***134 students*** in ***eleven states*** had been ***expelled*** for abstaining from the Pledge of Allegiance because of their beliefs.

Meanwhile, ***Roudabush*** heard that Lillian and William were being ***homeschooled*** and threatened that they ***"would be sent to reform school"*** if they were not taught by a ***professional*** teacher.

So the Gobitases, and several other local Jehovah's Witness families whose children had refused to pledge, set up a makeshift ***school*** at the ***Jones family farm*** thirty miles away.

Between twenty and forty students attended what was called the ***Jones Kingdom School.***

Given the ***distances*** and the ***poor quality*** of the local ***roads,*** many of the students, including ***Lillian*** and ***William,*** had to ***stay*** at the farm during the week.

The living conditions on the farm were ***so crowded*** with these new boarders that the children had to sleep ***three to a bed.***

At the bench trial, Roudabush was the school district's only witness.
Why shouldn't a few children be allowed to refrain from saluting the flag?
Because it would be demoralizing to the whole group. The tendency would be to spread.
In our mixed population where we have foreigners of every variety, it would be no time until they would form a dislike, a disregard for our flag and country.

Roudabush acknowledged that Lillian and William were ***"very good children,"*** but he described their parents' views as ***"perverted."*** Then the court heard from Walter, Lillian, and William.

Why didn't you salute the flag in the school?
Because it is contrary to God's law...
...in Exodus, Chapter 20, verses 4 to 7...
What does that say?
"Thou shalt not make unto thee any graven image, or any likeness of any thing that is in heaven above, or that is in the earth beneath, or that is in the water under the earth: Thou shalt not bow down thyself to them, nor serve them..."
In 1938, Judge Albert Maris ruled strongly in favor of the Gobitas family.
His opinion resoundingly rejected claims that it was necessary to make the pledge mandatory:

"Our country's safety surely does not depend upon the **totalitarian idea** of forcing all citizens into **one common mold** of thinking and acting or requiring them to render a **lip service** of loyalty in a manner which conflicts with their **sincere** religious convictions.
"Such a doctrine seems to me **utterly alien** to the genius and spirit of our nation and **destructive** of that **personal liberty** of which our flag itself is the **symbol.**"

The school district ***appealed*** the ruling, which caused the Witness children to remain ***shut out*** of the public schools.

SCHOOL

Five months later, the U.S. Court of Appeals for the Third Circuit ***unanimously affirmed*** the decision in favor of the Gobitases.

The Supreme Court agreed to hear the school district's final appeal, and oral argument took place on ***April 25, 1940.***

SEAL OF THE SUPREME COURT OF THE UNITED STATES

The justices' decision to take on the case was likely influenced by ***world events*** at that time.

As ***Nazi dominance*** in Europe continued to expand, the ***crucial issues*** involved in ***Minersville School District v. Gobitis***—

—***liberty, loyalty,*** and ***patriotism***—

—took on an even ***greater urgency.***

(The court misspelled Walter Gobitas's last name as "Gobitis," and the mistake would continue throughout their legal process all the way to the Supreme Court.)

Remarkably, the Witnesses' leader, ***Rutherford,*** who had practiced law earlier in his career, argued part of the case himself before the Court.

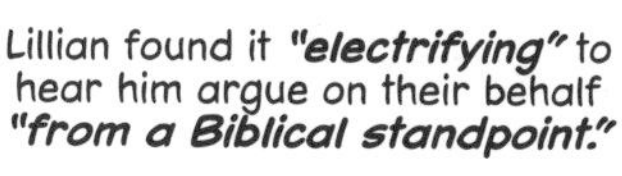
Lillian found it ***"electrifying"*** to hear him argue on their behalf ***"from a Biblical standpoint."***

George Gardner, a Harvard Law professor working on behalf of the ***American Civil Liberties Union*** (ACLU), put forth the more ***conventional*** legal position for the Gobitases, and focused on the ***religious liberty*** interests he advocated were ***protected*** by the ***First*** and ***Fourteenth Amendments.***

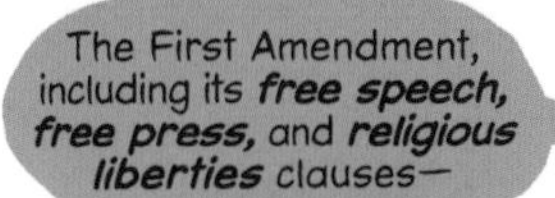

The First Amendment, including its *free speech, free press,* and *religious liberties* clauses—
—along with the rest of the *Bill of Rights*—
—was originally held to apply to *only* the *federal government* and *federal* laws.
Over *time,* the Supreme Court applied most of these fundamental protections, including all of the First Amendment, to *state action* and state laws as well.

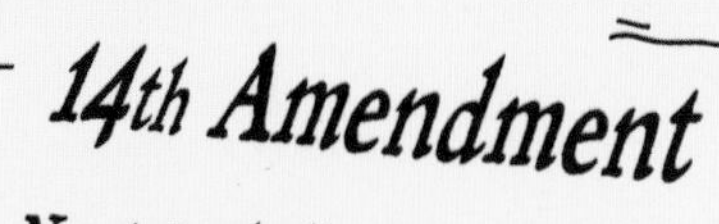
This *"incorporation doctrine"* interpreted the *language* of the Fourteenth Amendment's Due Process Clause as the *vehicle* for applying the guarantees of these amendments as binding on *the states.*
14th Amendment
No state shall ... deprive any person of life, liberty or property without due process of law

Back at the oral argument, things were not going well for ***Gardner.***

He was facing a ***barrage*** of questions from one of the Court's newest justices, ***Felix Frankfurter.***

Frankfurter was a ***Jewish immigrant*** from ***Vienna,*** who came to this country at age twelve, not speaking a word of English. As a young man he attended public school on the Lower East Side and then City College. He went on to graduate from Harvard Law School and became the ***first*** Jewish professor there, as well as a close confidant of ***President Franklin Roosevelt.***

His civil libertarian pedigree was beyond reproach.
Before joining the Court, he had defended the radical anarchists **Sacco** and **Vanzetti,** and was a cofounder of the **ACLU.**
ACLU
Everything in his background should have made him a natural ally for the Gobitas children.
However, any such expectations were about to be **upended** by the opinion he was going to write, over the same time period that **France** was falling to the **Nazis.**
Justice Frankfurter's majority opinion **reversed** the decisions of the lower courts and ruled in **favor** of the school district.
Frankfurter framed the issue at hand as a matter of balancing "conflicting claims of **liberty** and **authority**... Our present task... is to reconcile **two rights** in order to prevent either from **destroying** the other."
LIBERTY
AUTHORITY

For Frankfurter, the choice was clear. As the war in Europe threatened to engulf the world, ***religious freedom*** was outweighed in favor of the power of government to enforce ***patriotism,*** which he believed was ***"an interest inferior to none in the hierarchy of legal values."***

"National ***unity*** is the basis of national ***security.*** The ultimate foundation of a ***free society*** is the binding tie of ***cohesive sentiment,*** without which there can ultimately be no ***liberties,*** civil or religious."

Frankfurter also prioritized the ***flag*** over other symbols.

"The flag is the symbol of our ***national unity,*** transcending all internal differences, however large, within the framework of the Constitution."

Even assuming the "folly" of forcing students to recite the pledge ***against their will,*** Frankfurter insisted that the Courts must defer to ***local legislatures.***

To rule otherwise, he concluded, would inappropriately turn the Supreme Court into "the school board for the country."

Justice Harlan Fiske Stone was the lone ***dissenter.*** He held that First Amendment liberty guaranteed "the freedom of the individual from compulsion as to ***what he shall think and what he shall say."***

"History teaches us that there have been but ***few*** infringements of personal liberty by the state which have ***not*** been justified, as they are here, in the name of ***righteousness*** and the ***public good,*** and few which have not been directed, as they are now, at politically ***helpless minorities."***

In contrast to Frankfurter's view that liberty sometimes must be sacrificed for security, Stone saw the Constitution differently.
"It is," he urged, "an expression of faith and a command that freedom of mind and spirit must be preserved, which government must obey if it is to adhere to that justice and moderation without which no free government can exist."
Lillian Gobitas heard the news on the radio that the Supreme Court had decided her case, and that "it was against us, eight to one."
"Talk about a cold feeling! We absolutely did not expect that. That just set off a wave of persecution. It was like open season on Jehovah's Witnesses. That's when the mobs escalated."
The Gobitases' family store was threatened and then boycotted. Only a week after the case was decided, the Department of Justice had received complaints of hundreds of attacks on Jehovah's Witnesses.
Religious bigotry mixed with paranoia about Fifth Columnists (Nazi sympathizers seeking to undermine the country from within) led to horrific acts of violence across the country.

In **Maine,** mobs **set fire** to a local Kingdom Hall, the Jehovah's Witnesses' place of worship, **dragged** people from their homes, demanding they **salute the flag,** and **assaulted** them.
KINGDOM HALL OF JEHOVAH'S WITNESSES

CASTOR

In **West Virginia,** Jehovah's Witnesses were "rounded up and roped **like cattle**" by a sheriff's deputy and forced to drink **castor oil.**

In **Nebraska,** a Witness was **castrated.**

Another telling incident involved a report of four women and seven men who were marched out of a Southern town by a crowd throwing wood, rocks, and bricks at them.

When a **journalist** asked the sheriff what was happening, he replied, **"Jehovah's Witnesses...**They're running 'em out of here. They're **traitors**—the Supreme Court **says so.** Ain't you heard?"

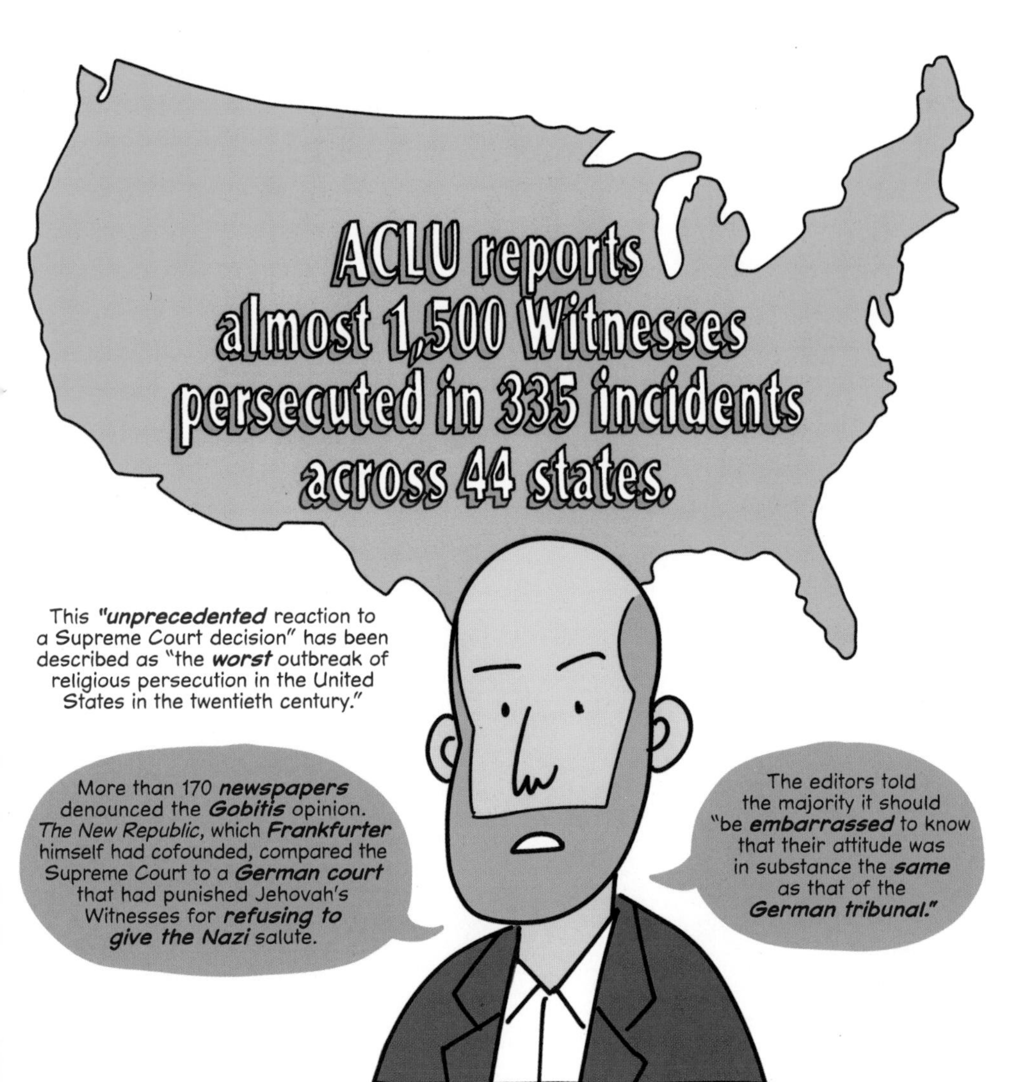
ACLU reports almost 1,500 Witnesses persecuted in 335 incidents across 44 states.
This "unprecedented reaction to a Supreme Court decision" has been described as "the worst outbreak of religious persecution in the United States in the twentieth century."
More than 170 newspapers denounced the Gobitis opinion. The New Republic, which Frankfurter himself had cofounded, compared the Supreme Court to a German court that had punished Jehovah's Witnesses for refusing to give the Nazi salute.
The editors told the majority it should "be embarrassed to know that their attitude was in substance the same as that of the German tribunal."

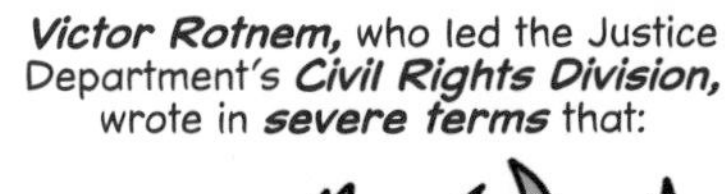
Victor Rotnem, who led the Justice Department's Civil Rights Division, wrote in severe terms that:

"This *ugly* picture of the two years following the *Gobitis* decision is an eloquent argument *in support* of the minority contention of Mr. Justice Stone.

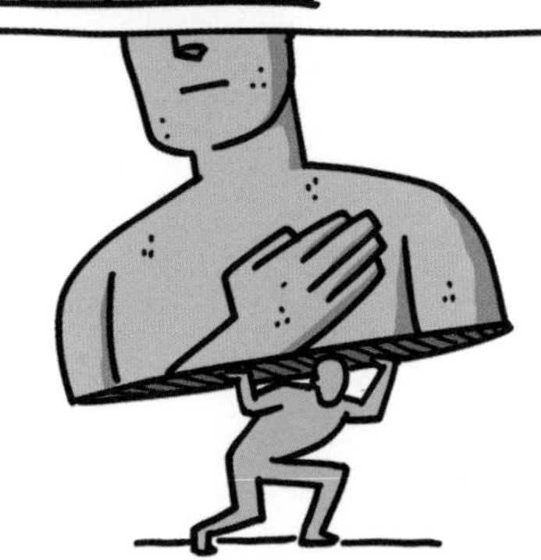

"The placing of *symbolic exercises* on a higher plane than *freedom of conscience* has made this symbol an instrument of *oppression* of a religious minority.

"The flag has been ***violated*** by its misuse
to deny the very ***freedoms*** it is intended to represent."
Within three years after the Court's ruling, about ***2,000 students,*** almost all of them Jehovah's Witnesses, in every state had been ***expelled*** for refusing to salute the flag.
SCHOOL
In some cases, ***parents*** of the expelled students were then ***prosecuted*** for violating mandatory school attendance laws.

In ***another*** First Amendment case involving Jehovah's Witnesses, ***Justices Hugo Black, William O. Douglas,*** and ***Frank Murphy*** stated in their dissent that "Since we joined in the opinion in the ***Gobitis*** case, we think this is an appropriate occasion to state that we now believe that it was also ***wrongly decided.***"
Douglas
Murphy
Black
Just for you...
In Supreme Court terms, this was the equivalent of an ***engraved invitation*** to ***revisit*** the case. The Jehovah's Witnesses' ***new*** national legal counsel, ***Hayden Covington,*** quickly responded by finding sympathetic new plaintiffs to lead just such a test case.

Marie Barnett was nine years old, raised as a Jehovah's Witness from birth, and attended Slip Hill Grade School in West Virginia with her sister, ***Gathie,*** age eleven.

The school didn't even have a flag, so they put up a ***picture*** of a flag. When we refused to salute it, they brought in a ***real*** flag to see if that would make any difference. We ***still*** refused.
[We] respect the flag and what it stands for. We don't have anything against that. We just don't believe in ***worshipping*** or ***saluting*** it.

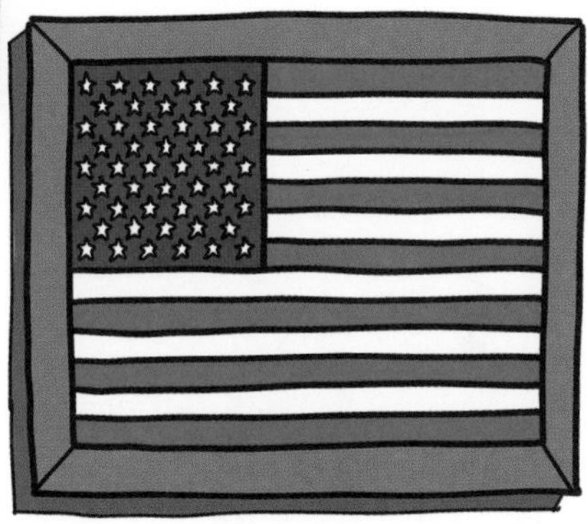

The Barnett sisters' ***classmates*** started calling them names once they stopped saluting the flag.

You're no better than the ***Japanese!***

After the bombing of ***Pearl Harbor,*** the country was quickly becoming swept up in intense feelings of ***fear, patriotism,*** and ***nationalistic fervor.***

A month after the United States entered the war, the West Virginia Board of Education passed a resolution that required teachers and students to participate in saluting the flag.

The language of the resolution drew directly from the ***Gobitis*** decision, and set forth that:
"Refusal to salute the flag [was to] be regarded as an act of insubordination, and shall be dealt with accordingly."
The consequences were shockingly ***severe.***

Students could be ***expelled*** and might be sentenced to live in reformatories for ***juvenile delinquents.***

Parents could face ***fines*** or up to thirty days in ***jail!***

Covington took up the Barnett sisters' case, along with five other children from two different families, all of whom had been ***expelled.***

The families sought a ***court order*** to stop the state board of education from enforcing the mandatory flag-salute resolution.
In the West Virginia federal district court, the Barnetts achieved a surprising ***victory.***

Ordinarily we would feel constrained to follow an unreversed decision of the Supreme Court of the United States, whether we agreed with it or not.
[However,] developments with respect to the Gobitis case...are such that we do not feel that it is incumbent upon us to accept it as binding authority.
Of the seven justices now members of the Supreme Court who participated in that decision, four have given public expression to the view that it is unsound.
Judge John Johnson Parker

The salute to the flag is an expression of the homage of the soul. To force it upon one who has conscientious scruples against giving it...
...is petty tyranny unworthy of the spirit of this Republic and forbidden... by the fundamental law.

As the West Virginia State Board of Education was appealing the decision, a major development in the history of the Pledge of Allegiance took place.

When the pledge was first created in 1892 by Christian socialist Francis Bellamy, the prescribed accompanying flag salute had a disturbing similarity to what would become the infamous Nazi "Heil Hitler" salute.

In December 1942, Congress acted to adopt a ***new*** recommended gesture.
Although this ***evolution*** in the mechanics of the flag salute had no ***direct impact*** on the Supreme Court's forthcoming ***West Virginia v. Barnette*** decision...
...redefining American liberties in stark contrast to ***fascism*** would prove a ***considerable*** factor in the ***constitutional shift*** to come.

(The Barnetts, like the Gobitases, had their last name misspelled in the case name of the Supreme Court decision with which they would be forever identified.)

By 1943, the ***lone dissenter*** in ***Gobitis, Harlan Stone,*** had become the chief justice.

There were now ***six votes*** to overturn ***Gobitis*** and ***prohibit*** compulsory flag salutes for public school students.

As chief justice, Stone had the power to decide ***who*** would write any decision in which he was in the majority.

He assigned the formidable task to a junior justice who had been on the Supreme Court for less than two years: ***Robert Jackson.***

The decision has been called "the most ***eloquent*** and ***enduring*** opinion in the Court's history."

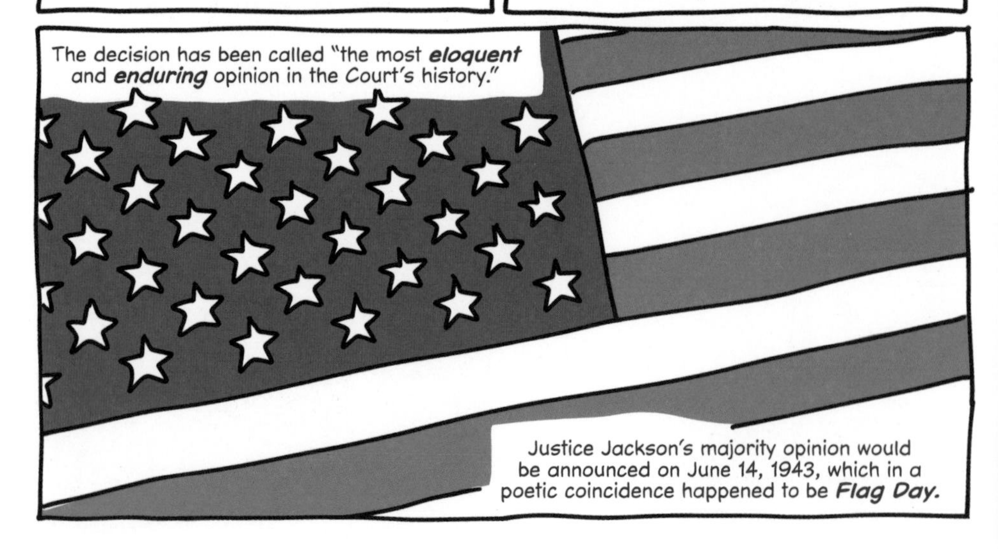

Justice Jackson's majority opinion would be announced on June 14, 1943, which in a poetic coincidence happened to be ***Flag Day.***

[The state] employs a ***flag*** as a symbol of adherence to government as presently organized.
It requires the individual to communicate ***by word*** and ***sign*** his acceptance of the political ideas it thus bespeaks.
Objection to this form of communication, when ***coerced,*** is an old one, ***well known*** to the framers of the ***Bill of Rights.***

"The ***Gobitis*** decision...***assumed...***that power exists in the State to impose the flag salute discipline upon school children in ***general.***

"The Court only examined and rejected a claim based on ***religious beliefs of immunity*** from an ***unquestioned general rule.***

"The question which ***underlies*** the flag salute controversy is whether such a ceremony so touching matters of ***opinion*** and ***political attitude*** may be imposed upon the individual by official authority under powers committed to ***any*** political organization under our Constitution."

In this ***masterstroke,*** Jackson ***transforms*** the question from whether Jehovah's Witnesses should be granted a religious exception to a presumptively valid rule, to whether there is a ***free speech right*** for ***all citizens*** to be protected from compelled speech in the ***first place.***

"To ***sustain*** the compulsory flag salute, we are required to say that a ***Bill of Rights*** which guards the individual's right to speak his own mind left it ***open*** to public authorities to compel him to utter what is ***not*** in his mind."

BILL OF RIGHTS

The right to ***remain silent,*** the Supreme Court recognized for the first time, is an ***inherent*** part of free speech.
Jackson also vigorously rejected Frankfurter's arguments in ***Gobitis*** for judicial restraint and deference to state legislatures.

BILL OF RIGHTS

"The very ***purpose*** of a Bill of Rights was to ***withdraw*** certain subjects from the vicissitudes of political controversy, to place them ***beyond the reach*** of majorities and officials, and to establish them as legal principles to be applied by the courts."

In no uncertain terms, Jackson makes clear the ***vital role*** judicial review plays as a check on the political process:

"One's right to ***life, liberty,*** and ***property,*** to ***free speech,*** a ***free press, freedom of worship*** and ***assembly,*** and other fundamental rights may not be submitted to vote; they depend on the outcome of ***no elections.***"

NEWS

Dismantling Frankfurter's argument at "the very heart of the ***Gobitis*** opinion," that the need for ***"national unity"*** trumped other First Amendment interests was Jackson's ***next step.***

"National unity, as an end which officials may foster by ***persuasion*** and ***example,*** is not in question. The problem is whether, under our Constitution, ***compulsion*** as here employed is a ***permissible means*** for its achievement.

"Ultimate ***futility*** of such attempts to compel coherence is the lesson of every such effort from the Roman drive to stamp out Christianity as a disturber of its pagan unity...down to the fast failing efforts of our present ***totalitarian enemies.***

"Those who begin coercive ***elimination of dissent*** soon find themselves exterminating ***dissenters.*** Compulsory unification of opinion achieves only the ***unanimity of the graveyard."***

In his exquisitely expressed conclusion, Justice Jackson shows that the path to avoiding the deadly results of ***fascism*** can be found only by ***remaining true*** to our First Amendment values:

"It seems trite but necessary to say that the ***First Amendment*** to our Constitution was designed to avoid these ***ends*** by avoiding these ***beginnings.*** There is no ***mysticism*** in the American concept of the State or of the nature or origin of its authority.

"We set up government ***by consent of the governed,*** and the Bill of Rights denies those in power any legal opportunity to coerce that consent.

"Authority here is to be controlled ***by public opinion,*** not public opinion by authority. The case is made difficult not because the principles of its decision are ***obscure,*** but because the ***flag*** involved is our ***own.***

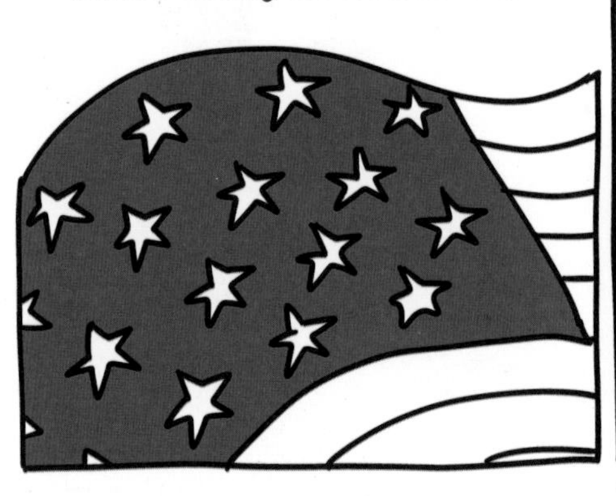

"Nevertheless, we apply the limitations of the Constitution with no fear that freedom to be intellectually and spiritually diverse or even contrary will disintegrate the social organization.

"If there is any fixed star in our constitutional constellation, it is that no official, high or petty, can prescribe what shall be orthodox in politics, nationalism, religion, or other matters of opinion, or force citizens to confess by word or act their faith therein."

Accordingly, the Court held that the West Virginia flag-salute regulation "invades the sphere of ***intellect*** and ***spirit*** which it is the purpose of the First Amendment to our Constitution to reserve from all official control," affirmed the lower court judgment putting an end to its enforcement, and ***overruled Gobitis.***

In a ***furious*** dissent, Justice Frankfurter ***doubled down*** on his insistence that ***Gobitis*** was rightly decided. He reserved his ***greatest ire*** for the lack of deference to ***state lawmakers*** and the majority's willingness to overturn such a ***recent*** precedent.

Frankfurter could not forgive them for rejecting the judicial principle of stare decisis, which is Latin for "to stand by things decided," and lies at the heart of our judicial system.

Of course, even he acknowledged that stare decisis was not absolute, and that sometimes the Supreme Court should change course and overturn a past decision.
DETOUR

However, the ***timing*** of overturning ***Gobitis***—in just ***three years***—was indeed highly unusual.

The ***Barnette*** decision was greeted with ***unbridled enthusiasm*** from the press.

TIME
We the People
Blot Removed.

The ***wartime*** nature of the decision was also crucial in elevating its reception.

Cornell Law School Professor Steven Shiffrin

Barnette was written in the midst of ***World War II,*** a time when America's self-understanding was that it was fighting to ***preserve democracy.*** It is illuminating that the Court would call forth the idea of ***protecting dissent*** as fundamental to what the society stood for.

As a result of Barnette, most schools across the United States quickly abandoned punishments for those who would not pledge allegiance to the flag.
And the Barnett sisters lost only a half of a year at school.
The Minersville School District informed the Gobitas family that their children were permitted to resume attending public school.
But it had been eight years since Lillian and William had been expelled, and they were now twenty and eighteen years old, respectively.
I would do it again in a second...
...without reservations!
Lillian Gobitas
The complex path to Barnette ends with an arrival at a clear free speech principle:
The government is restricted from compelling its citizens to express a message they don't support.
But what does this mean for Colin Kaepernick?

In early 2019, Kaepernick and Reid entered into a settlement with the NFL.
It had been two and a half years since their Take a Knee protests had sought to expose issues of racial injustice.
Although the NFL admitted no wrongdoing as part of the confidential agreement, it's still hard to view the deal (which almost certainly involved a substantial financial payout) as anything but at least a partial victory for the former player.
CONFIDENTIAL
Colin Kaepernick v. NFL
Despite being excluded from the NFL, his status as an icon of determination and dissent continued to rise.
When Nike made Kaepernick the spokesperson for its thirtieth anniversary "Just Do It" campaign and signed him to a lucrative expanded endorsement contract, he proved that commercial partnerships could amplify a protest message.

The fact that Barnette does not directly prevent the NFL, as a private business, from disciplining its players for their speech on the field, does not lessen its impact on the Take a Knee protests in two significant ways.
NFL

First, as the ***Take a Knee*** protests swept through professional sports, ***student*** athletes were also inspired to engage in their own protests during the national anthem at high school or college games.

32
22
8

Public schools at ***all*** educational levels are considered the ***equivalent*** of governmental actors for constitutional purposes. Protesting public school students are therefore ***squarely protected*** by ***Barnette.***

Second, Barnette provides an ***instructive guide*** as we grapple with whether ***protesting*** is in fact at the ***core*** of our patriotism for a country founded in revolution.

Like the ***Jehovah's Witnesses*** in the ***Gobitis*** and ***Barnette*** cases, ***Kaepernick*** faced ***unrelenting attacks*** on his patriotism based on ***three arguments:*** The protests were ***unpopular,*** done in the ***wrong place*** and ***manner,*** and ***disrespected*** the flag.

Polls taken throughout the controversy showed a ***theoretical*** support for free speech, while the Take a Knee protests themselves remained ***unpopular*** among a ***majority*** of Americans.

RIGHT TO NONVIOLENT PROTEST — *79% AGREE*

PROTECT RIGHTS OF THOSE WITH UNPOPULAR VIEWS — *74% AGREE*

TAKE A KNEE PROTEST IS UNPATRIOTIC — *72% AGREE*

One explanation could be that ***objection*** to the protests, as Trump puts it, "has nothing to do with ***race.*** It is about ***respect*** for our ***Country, Flag*** and ***National Anthem.***"

RESPECT

This viewpoint may seem somewhat plausible given that today, ***civil rights protests*** of the ***past*** are looked at with a rosy aura of ***moral authority*** and inevitability.
However, in the weeks before the ***1963 March on Washington,*** 60% of Americans viewed the protest ***unfavorably*** and only 23% looked on it ***favorably.***
MALCOLM X
WE MARCH FOR
NO U.S. DOUGH TO HELP JIM CROW GROW
WE MARCH FOR JOBS FOR ALL NOW!
Three years later, even the Reverend Dr. Martin Luther King Jr. was viewed ***negatively*** by ***63%*** of Americans!
It seems then that protest speech in the ***abstract*** is often ***highly praised,*** and yet in ***practice*** protesting and protest leaders are often ***feared*** and ***rejected,*** particularly when it concerns ***racial justice.***

Ta-Nehisi Coates has written that popularity was not the issue and that civil rights activists of the past actually "never successfully connected with the hearts of the majority of adults of their own day."

Instead, the civil rights movement succeeded because those engaged in civil disobedience "affected the attitudes of the ***children*** of those white Americans who scorned them.

"This points to the ***true target,*** in terms of white people, of Kaepernick's protest.

Ta-Nehisi Coates

"The point is ***not*** to convince people who boo even when a team kneels ***before*** the anthem is sung. The point is to reach the ***children*** of those people. The point is the ***future.***"

The ***second critique*** claims that the Take a Knee protests could have better shown their patriotism to white NFL audiences by somehow protesting ***differently.***

Progressive Christian pastor and author ***John Pavlovitz*** has dubbed this the "protest the 'right way'" argument. And he has characterized such comments as "the arrogant heart of privilege: being the beneficiaries of systematic injustice, and then wanting to make the rules for the marginalized in how they should speak into that injustice."

John Pavlovitz

And as ***Kareem Abdul-Jabbar*** discussed in an editorial for *The Guardian*, protesting during NFL games wasn't ***incidental*** for the players' protest, but rather "the ***perfect public platform*** for discussing racial disparity."

The NFL's significant ratings means it reaches not just a lot of people (an average of 18m), but a ***wider cross-section*** of people, particularly those whose hearts and minds ***need*** to be changed if we are to see ***progress.*** This target audience may not be ***aware*** of the problem or are reluctant to ***believe*** there is a problem until they see their favorite players week after week expressing their ***sadness and frustration*** at calculated ***government inaction.***

Kareem Abdul-Jabbar

THE HERITAGE
BLACK ATHLETES, A DIVIDED AMERICA, AND THE POLITICS OF PATRIOTISM
HOWARD BRYANT

The ***final*** critique of the Take a Knee protests is that they are inescapably ***unpatriotic*** because they come during a time set aside to ***honor the flag.***

Howard Bryant

Trump positioned dissenting views as ***unpatriotic*** at best, ***traitorous*** at worst, to both the United States in general and the country's armed forces in particular. The American flag did not represent ***ideals.*** It was supposed to be ***obeyed.***

On this point, the story of ***Barnette*** teaches us precisely how respect for the flag does not take precedence over First Amendment rights.

If the United States Supreme Court could bring itself to ***support*** the free speech of ***flag dissenters*** during the dark days of World War II, we can still follow their lead in ***today's*** unsettled times.

Of course, Kaepernick was not without defenders of his patriotism.
It baffles me that our protest is still being misconstrued as disrespectful to the country, flag and military personnel.
We chose it because it's exactly the opposite.
It has always been my understanding that the brave men and women who fought and died for our country did so to ensure that we could live in a fair and free society, which includes the right to speak out in protest.
Eric Reid
PROTES
It should go without saying that I love my country and I'm proud to be an American. But, to quote James Baldwin, "exactly for this reason, I insist on the right to criticize her perpetually."
And then, almost four years after Kaepernick first took a knee, George Floyd was killed on camera. Black Lives Matter protests in the wake of the deaths of Floyd, Breonna Taylor, and so many other Black people at the hands of police have finally moved many white people to realize how right and necessary Kaepernick's actions were.
No matter the shifting tides of popular opinion, the Barnette decision stands with Kaepernick as a persuasive ally in the fight to recognize that allowing for dissent—be it from Jehovah's Witnesses or football players—is the greatest and most patriotic of American values.
"To believe that patriotism will not flourish if patriotic ceremonies are voluntary and spontaneous, instead of a compulsory routine, is to make an unflattering estimate of the appeal of our institutions to free minds.... freedom to differ is not limited to things that do not matter much. That would be a mere shadow of freedom. The test of its substance is the right to differ as to things that touch the heart of the existing order."
Justice Robert Jackson

Chapter 3:
LIBEL, ACTUAL MALICE, AND THE CIVIL RIGHTS MOVEMENT

One of candidate Trump's more surprising campaign promises was his vow to "open up our libel laws." At a 2016 Texas rally during the Republican primary, as he launched into a familiar attack on the media, it soon took an unexpected turn:
TRUMP PENCE
I'll tell you what, I think the media is among the most dishonest groups of people I've ever met. And believe me, if I become president, oh, do they have problems. They're going to have such problems.
NEWSROOM
I'm going to open up our libel laws so when they write purposely negative and horrible and false articles, we can sue them and win lots of money.
So we're going to open up those libel laws, folks, and we're going to have people sue you like you never got sued before.

Although it is ***hard*** to imagine ***any*** cross section of the American public that would consider ***libel law*** a pressing ***concern,*** this is nevertheless a ***theme*** that President Trump returned to ***over and over*** again.

Lashing out against the publication of ***Michael Wolff's*** scathing book *Fire and Fury: Inside the Trump White House*, Trump declared that:

We are going to take a strong look at our country's libel laws so that when somebody says something that is...***totally false and knowingly false,*** that the person who has been abused, defamed, libeled, will have ***meaningful recourse.***

He returned to this refrain again in reaction to the release of ***Bob Woodward's*** book, *Fear: Trump in the White House*, tweeting that:

Isn't it a shame that someone can write an article or book, totally make up stories and form a picture of a person that is literally the exact opposite of the fact, and get away with it without retribution or cost. Don't know why Washington politicians don't change libel laws?

Within the next six months, ***Justice Clarence Thomas*** followed Trump's lead and similarly called for a reconsideration of the constitutional foundations of modern libel law.

Justice Clarence Thomas

He criticized the Supreme Court's past precedents as "policy-driven decisions masquerading as constitutional law."

LAW

Thomas chided that the Court "did not begin meddling in this area until 1964, nearly 175 years after the First Amendment was ratified."

For Thomas, this ***gap*** indicates that the Court has ***strayed too far*** from what the framers of the Constitution thought about libel at the time of its enactment.

MAP
YOU ARE HERE
(LOST)
START

Instead, he advocated for the Court to adopt his ***originalist approach*** and "carefully examine the original meaning" of the First Amendment.

If the framers did not understand the Constitution as requiring "public figures to satisfy an actual-malice standard in state-law defamation suits, then neither should we."

Do libel laws allow the press to say things that are ***"totally false"*** and get away with it? ***Can*** politicians change libel law? What does ***actual malice*** really mean? The answers to all of these questions can be explained by looking back at the foundational case of ***New York Times Company v. Sullivan.***
NYT VS. SULLIVAN

Sullivan is the source of the widely ***misunderstood*** actual malice test, which extended First Amendment protection for the first time to even ***false statements*** criticizing public figures.

The New York Times

Sullivan is the story of how a Southern libel judgment against an ad supporting the ***Reverend Dr. Martin Luther King Jr.*** almost bankrupted *The New York Times*, but resulted in a Supreme Court decision that saved the paper and provided a pivotal ***victory*** for the ***civil rights*** movement.

In March of 1960, student-led sit-in protests of ***segregated lunch counters*** had spread across the South. At the same time as ***Dr. King*** was supporting the student actions, he was preparing to defend himself against felony ***perjury*** charges for allegedly making ***false statements*** in connection with his Alabama state tax returns.

Meanwhile in ***New York,*** a ***Committee to Defend Martin Luther King and the Struggle for Freedom in the South*** was formed at the home of singer and civil rights activist ***Harry Belafonte,*** to raise money to provide for his legal defense.
On March 29, the Committee took out a full-page advertisement in *The New York Times* to support the student demonstrations and ***condemn*** the actions taken against the activists and Dr. King.
Heed Their Rising Voices
Your Help Is Urgently Needed . . . NOW !!
COMMITTEE TO DEFEND MARTIN LUTHER KING AND THE STRUGGLE FOR FREEDOM IN THE SOUTH

The ad began by paying tribute to the "thousands of Southern Negro students [that] are engaged in wide-spread non-violent demonstrations in positive affirmation of the right to live in human dignity as guaranteed by the U.S. Constitution and the Bill of Rights." It also highlighted some of the ***nonviolent*** actions taken by students, the ***terrorizing*** responses they faced in Montgomery, Alabama, and other Southern cities, and how Dr. King "has inspired and guided the students in their widening wave of sit-ins."

The ad copy went on to describe Dr. King's plight:

"Again and again the Southern violators have answered Dr. King's peaceful protests with intimidation and violence.
"They have bombed his home almost killing his wife and child. They have assaulted his person. They have arrested him seven times—for 'speeding,' 'loitering,' and similar 'offenses.'
"And now they have charged him with 'perjury'—a *felony* under which they could imprison him for ten *years*.
"Obviously, their real purpose is to remove him physically as the leader to whom the students and millions of others look for guidance and support, and thereby to intimidate all leaders who may rise in the South.
"The defense of Martin Luther King, spiritual leader of the student sit-in movement, clearly, therefore, is an integral part of the total struggle for freedom in the South."
Please mail this coupon TODAY!
Committee To Defend Martin Luther King
and
The Struggle For Freedom In The South.
312 West 125th Street, New York 27, N. Y.
University 6-1700
The committee urgently requested donations (via a mail-in coupon) for "this Combined Appeal for all three needs—the defense of Martin Luther King—the support of the embattled students—and the struggle for the right-to-vote."

The request was signed by ***sixty-four*** civil rights activists and celebrities.

Underneath these individuals were the names of twenty Southerners, nearly all ***clergymen,*** "who are struggling daily for dignity and freedom [and] warmly endorse this appeal."

Harry Belafonte
Marlon Brando
Diahann Carroll
Nat King Cole
Dorothy Dandridge
Sammy Davis Jr.
Lorraine Hansbury
Langston Hughes
Mahalia Jackson
Eartha Kitt
Rabbi Edward Klein
John Lewis
Sidney Poitier
A. Philip Randolph
Jackie Robinson
Eleanor Roosevelt

Only 394 copies of the newspaper containing the advertisement were distributed in ***Alabama*** (out of a circulation of about 650,000 copies nationally), but the ***reaction*** from ***state officials*** was fast and furious.

L. B. Sullivan, a city commissioner of Montgomery, wrote to the *Times* ten days later demanding a ***full retraction.*** Although not named in the ad, Sullivan claimed that it accused him of ***"grave misconduct"*** and ***"improper actions"*** as a city official.

The *Times* responded to Sullivan that it was "somewhat puzzled as to how you think the statements reflect on you" and that the advertisement was ***"substantially correct."***

The New York Times

Sullivan promptly brought a ***libel lawsuit*** against *The New York Times* and the four Black ministers from Alabama whose names were listed as endorsing the appeal—the Reverends Ralph Abernathy, Fred Shuttlesworth, S. S. Seay Sr., and J. E. Lowery. He sought ***$500,000*** in damages.

The governor of Alabama, ***John Patterson,*** who was also ***not named*** in the ad, soon followed with a copycat retraction demand.

This time, the *Times* ***backtracked,*** apologized, and retracted the paragraphs that referred to Montgomery and the arrests of Dr. King by "Southern violators" for containing ***factual inaccuracies.***

The New York Times.

Nevertheless, Governor Patterson sued the *Times* and the ministers for libel as well, but he included ***Dr. King*** as an additional defendant. Not to be outdone, the governor asked for ***$1 million*** in damages.

The *Times,* along with Abernathy, Shuttlesworth, Seay, and Lowery, would be sued ***again*** for libel by the mayor of Montgomery, another city commissioner, and a former city commissioner, demanding $500,000 each.

That meant the defendants were facing damage claims of ***$3 million*** in total (approximately ***25 million*** in today's dollars) for publishing a single political advertisement.

The New York Times.

In the wake of this litigation onslaught, the *Times'* counsel ***Louis Loeb*** later said, "In all the years I have practiced law...***nothing*** scared me more than this litigation."

Louis Loeb

Who were L. B. Sullivan and John Patterson, and why were they seemingly so upset by the advertisement? Sullivan was a member of the Ku Klux Klan, and his campaign for city commissioner attacked the incumbent for using "kid gloves to handle social agitators" like Dr. King.
As attorney general of Alabama, Patterson sought and won a court order to effectively ban the National Association for the Advancement of Colored People (NAACP) within the entire state. (It would take the NAACP multiple trips to the Supreme Court over eight years to overturn these prohibitions.)
L. B. Sullivan
John Patterson

Just one month prior to the publication of "Heed Their Rising Voices," Governor Patterson would demand the ***expulsion*** of thirty-five Black students from Alabama State College for participating in a ***sit-in protest*** at the segregated snack bar in the Montgomery County Courthouse.

It is therefore ***hard to believe*** that Sullivan or Patterson ***truly*** felt their reputations were damaged by being criticized by Black civil rights advocates. To the contrary, their political fortunes had been madein large part on taking an aggressively ***segregationist stance.***

There could be little doubt that these cases were ***not*** about vindicating real reputational injury, but rather were a thinly veiled effort to attack civil rights activists.

Reverend
Ralph
Abernathy
Reverend
Fred
Shuttlesworth
Reverend
J. E. Lowery
Reverend
S. S.
Seay Sr.

The minister defendants were at the forefront of the civil rights movement. Abernathy, Shuttlesworth, and Lowery were ***cofounders,*** along with Dr. King, of the ***Southern Christian Leadership Conference.*** Seay was one of the ***leading organizers*** of the Montgomery bus boycott, and all of them were among Dr. King's ***closest*** confidants and advisers.

Presiding over Sullivan's libel trial against the *Times* and the ministers was ***Judge Walter Burgwyn Jones.*** Judge Jones maintained strictly ***segregated*** courtroom seating. He had also spoken of his admiration for "white man's justice, a justice born long centuries ago in England, brought over to this country by the Anglo-Saxon race."

Perhaps not surprisingly then, from a panel of thirty-six potential jurors, only ***two*** were Black, and both were successfully challenged by Sullivan's lawyer, so that an ***all-white*** jury was selected.

At every libel trial, the ***plaintiff*** has to prove ***four crucial elements:*** that the statements at issue were about the ***plaintiff,*** were ***false,*** injured the plaintiff's ***reputation,*** and were made ***publicly*** by the defendant. To establish this, Sullivan claimed that this paragraph mentioning Montgomery police was referring to him, given his supervisory role over the department:

"In Montgomery, Alabama, after students sang 'My Country, 'Tis of Thee' on the State Capitol steps, their leaders were expelled from school, and truck-loads of police armed with shotguns and tear-gas ringed the Alabama State College Campus. When the entire student body protested to state authorities by refusing to re-register, their dining hall was pad-locked in an attempt to starve them into submission."

M. Roland Nachman

Sullivan also maintained that the reference to ***"Southern violators"*** arresting Dr. King implicated him as well. Sullivan's lawyer, ***M. Roland Nachman,*** called six witnesses who said they associated these statements with Sullivan and that if they had believed the statements it would have ***damaged*** their opinion of him.

On cross-examination, ***five*** of the witnesses admitted they ***never saw*** the ad until ***Nachman*** had shown it to them in preparation for trial and ***none*** of them believed the statements.

As for the issue of falsity, some minor factual errors in the paragraphs at issue were established. There was ***no evidence*** that the Alabama State College dining hall had been padlocked, and Dr. King had been arrested not ***seven*** times, but "only" ***four.***

Finally, Abernathy, Shuttlesworth, Seay, and Lowery testified that they had ***no knowledge*** of the ad until ***after*** it was published. The ad's ***author*** supported this, saying that their names had been added at the last minute ***without*** their ***permission,*** because there wasn't ***time*** to reach them.

Their attorney, famed civil rights litigator ***Fred Gray,*** sought to have the ministers ***removed*** from the case.

There was not a ***scintilla*** of evidence against our clients.

They had ***no knowledge*** of the advertisement. They had ***not written it.*** They had never ***seen it.*** They did not know their ***names*** would be in it.

Judge Jones denied *Gray's* motion.

The jury took a little more than two hours to find in favor of Sullivan. The twelve white men awarded him the entire $500,000 he had asked for in damages. It was the ***largest*** libel award in the history of Alabama.

The reaction of the ***local press*** was euphoric.

"[The] half-million dollar judgment...could have the effect of causing reckless publishers of the North...to make a re-survey of their habit of permitting anything detrimental to the South and its people to appear in their columns."

—*The Alabama Journal*

"State Finds Formidable Legal Club to Swing at Out-of-State Press."

—*The Montgomery Advertiser*

Another libel victory with ***another*** award of $500,000 in damages followed a few months later—this time in the suit brought by the mayor. With the looming threat of ***three more*** pending suits over the advertisement, their cumulative impact could have ***bankrupted*** the newspaper.
The New York Times
"Without a ***reversal*** of those verdicts there was a reasonable question of whether the *Times...* could survive."
Louis Loeb

Sullivan also ***financially attacked*** the minister defendants by ***seizing*** their ***property,*** ostensibly to pay for the damages they would owe if and when the court judgment became final.

The plaintiff in this case was so determined to ***punish*** African Americans who identified with the movement that his attorneys... did not have the ***human decency*** to wait until the appeal was ***over*** before levying on the ministers' property.

Fred Gray

The financial impact on ***Dr. King*** was equally pronounced. Fundraising for King through advertising had been ***crippled.***

PARTING THE WATERS
AMERICA IN THE KING YEARS 1954-63
TAYLOR BRANCH
Taylor Branch
The white authorities of Alabama were serving notice that newspapers willing to publish King's paid messages had to fear that Alabama might haul them into court.

Perhaps most seriously, the strategy of ***censorship*** by libel threats was working.

[The press] was ***essential*** to the conduct of non-violent demonstrations... It was ***no accident*** that our demonstrations were always in the ***morning***...so that we could make the ***evening news;*** and so that reports could file their deadlines for the coming day.

Civil rights leader ***Andrew Young***

Without press coverage, the ***impact*** of the movement would be ***thwarted.***

By the time the Alabama Supreme Court had ***affirmed*** the trial court ruling in 1962, the *Times* had kept its reporters ***away*** from Alabama and relied on wire services for more than a ***year.***
The New York T

The threats were also ***spreading.***

THE RACE BEAT
GENE ROBERTS AND HANK KLIBANO

Journalists ***Gene Roberts*** and ***Hank Klibanoff***

"Public officials in three southern states had no fewer than seventeen libel lawsuits pending against newspapers, magazines, and a television station, seeking total damages that exceeded $288 million. The court would decide nothing less than how free the press really could be. If the decision went against the *Times*, would reporters be vulnerable to every libel claim filed by a ticked-off sheriff?"

In the legal briefs leading up to the Supreme Court oral argument, the defendants took strikingly ***different*** approaches.

The *New York Times* team, led by Columbia Law School professor ***Herbert Wechsler,*** focused almost entirely on the ***free press*** and ***free speech*** issues involved—criticism of government officials is ***essential*** to the ***First Amendment,*** and state libel laws should not be allowed to undermine that freedom.

Herbert Wechsler

Whereas the ministers' brief called out the ***racism*** of the trial and society in no uncertain terms:

"Where Sullivan, a white public official, sued Negro petitioners represented by Negro counsel before an all-white jury, in Montgomery, Alabama, on an advertisement seeking to aid the cause of integration, the impact of courtroom segregation could only denote the inferiority of Negroes and taint and infect all proceedings thereby denying petitioners the fair and impartial trial to which they are constitutionally entitled."

Interestingly, King's counsel "concurred in the suppression of the racial aspects" as a matter of "strategic realism." Recognizing that the Court would be unwilling to take the systemic racism of Alabama government head-on, King's team instead sought to appeal to "anyone who could imagine being victimized by parochial politics or a runaway jury."

Dr. Martin Luther King Jr.

The Court was hearing the oral arguments for ***Sullivan*** at a ***traumatic*** and ***fragile time*** in the history of American democracy. Only forty-five days after the ***assassination*** of ***President Kennedy*** and six months before the passage of the ***Civil Rights Act of 1964,*** Wechsler began with a dramatic opening that fit the times.

The ***Sullivan*** libel decision posed ***"hazards*** to the ***freedom of the press*** of a dimension not confronted since the early days as the Republic."

Wechsler's main argument was that "the First Amendment was ***precisely*** designed to do away with...punishment for criticism of the ***Government*** and criticism of ***officials,"*** and therefore the First Amendment must limit the ability of state libel laws to punish such criticism.

If the Court did not impose free speech constraints on state libel law, massive damage awards like those in Sullivan would be "a death penalty for any newspaper if multiplied."

Representing the ministers was ***Samuel R. Pierce Jr.,*** a former judge and the first Black partner of a prominent New York law firm. Pierce was arguing before ***Justice Hugo Black,*** the most senior member of the Court and a former member of the ***Ku Klux Klan.*** Pierce got to the ***heart*** of the case that Wechsler and Nachman both strenuously ***avoided:***

Samuel R. Pierce Jr.
Justice Hugo Black

"The sole purpose of this litigation is to suppress and punish expressions of support for the cause of racial equality and to try to keep those who are actively engaged in their fight for civil rights, such as the [ministers] in this case from continuing to participate in that struggle."

"The injustice of this action which encroaches on freedom of speech under the guise of punishing for libel is magnified by the fact that the petitioners failed to receive a fair trial."

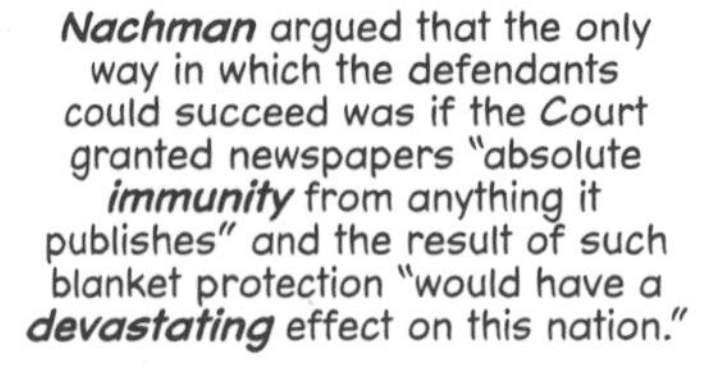

Nachman argued that the only way in which the defendants could succeed was if the Court granted newspapers "absolute ***immunity*** from anything it publishes" and the result of such blanket protection "would have a ***devastating*** effect on this nation."

He went so far as to say that even if a newspaper had "a reasonable belief" in the truth of what it published, it would still be subject to ***punishment*** under Alabama law if any statement turned out ***not*** to be fully ***accurate.***

Justice William J. Brennan labored over ***eight drafts*** of his opinion in order to ultimately get all nine justices to agree on a decision in favor of *The New York Times.*

The ***unanimous*** judgment for the defendants meant that Sullivan's libel victory was going to be ***taken away*** from him, but on what ***grounds?***

YANK!

Brennan's opinion for the Court telegraphed that ***sweeping change*** was to follow:

"We consider this case against the background of a profound ***national commitment*** to the principle that ***debate*** on public issues should be ***uninhibited, robust,*** and ***wide open,*** and that it may well include ***vehement, caustic,*** and sometimes unpleasantly ***sharp attacks*** on government and public officials.

"Erroneous statement is ***inevitable*** in free debate, and [therefore sometimes even false statements] must be ***protected*** if the freedoms of expression are to have the breathing space that they need to ***survive.***"

FALSE

Given this inevitable potential for ***error,*** the consequences of allowing the status quo to continue were presented in stark terms of ***survival.***

"Whether or not a newspaper can survive a ***succession*** of such judgments, the pall of ***fear*** and ***timidity*** imposed upon those who would give voice to ***public criticism*** is an atmosphere in which the First Amendment freedoms ***cannot survive.***

The New York Times

"Under such a rule, would-be critics of official conduct may be ***deterred*** from voicing their criticism, even though it is believed to be true and even though it is, in fact, true, because of ***doubt*** whether it can be proved in court or fear of the expense of having to do so."

Brennan had laid out the conflict between ***free speech*** and ***libel law,*** and why a ***new standard*** for both interests was vital. If libel litigation must now be curtailed by the First Amendment, Brennan then proclaimed what this new limitation would be—an ***actual malice*** requirement.

"The constitutional guarantees require," Brennan set forth, "a **federal rule** that prohibits a public official from recovering damages for [libel] unless he proves that the statement was made with ***'actual malice'***—that is, with ***knowledge*** that it was ***false*** or with ***reckless disregard*** of whether it was false or not."
Brennan found that the defendants did ***not*** make any statements with reckless disregard of the truth, even if some of those statements in the advertisement were false and could have been checked more thoroughly.
Heed Their Rising Voices
Your Help Is Urgently Needed . . . NOW!!
The decision went on to hold that the advertisement was also insufficiently ***"of and concerning"*** Sullivan in that an "impersonal attack on governmental operations," cannot in and of itself constitute libel of an ***unnamed*** "official responsible for those operations."

For both of these reasons, the libel decision of the Alabama Supreme Court was ***reversed*** and all of the defendants had now won a ***breathtaking triumph.***

In crafting the ***actual malice*** test, Brennan sought to strike a balance between ***blanket protection*** for all incorrect statements and ***no protection*** for any inaccuracies.

Immunity
OPEN SEASON

Contrary to popular belief, the actual malice standard does not have anything to do with ***ill will*** or ***bad intent.***

What this meant, and ***continues*** to mean, for journalists is that they need not be ***infallible,*** but they can't ***make stuff up*** ("knowledge that it was false") and they also can't ***turn a blind eye*** to the ***truth*** or contradictory information ("reckless disregard").

The decision was met almost immediately with ***rapturous enthusiasm,*** with a prominent philosopher and free speech advocate hailing it as "an occasion for dancing in the streets."

Thirty years later, when ***Justice Elena Kagan*** was a professor of law at the University of Chicago, she wrote that "the decision speaks to the widest possible audience [and] as a statement of enduring principle addressed to the American people—it is indeed a ***marvel.***"

On the fiftieth anniversary of ***Sullivan,*** *The Atlantic* magazine published a tribute for the occasion in modern terms:

THE NEWS

"Every person who writes ***online*** or otherwise about public officials, every hack or poet who criticizes the work of government, every ***distinguished journalist*** or ***pajama-ed blogger*** who speaks ***truth to power,*** ought to bow his or her head today in a silent moment of ***gratitude*** for [the ***Sullivan*** decision]. It means simply that you can make an ***honest mistake*** when writing about a public figure and won't likely get sued."

However, on ***closer*** examination, how can the ***protection of the press*** be treated as a victory for speech or justice when, as Professor Catharine A. MacKinnon frames it, the ***"civil rights speech*** at the case's factual foundation [was] ***ignored,*** [and] the Court proceeded as if the ***underlying substantive inequality*** between ***assertion*** of civil rights and official Southern police ***suppression*** of their ***pursuit***...was irrelevant..."?

There are no easy answers to this type of critique. While the debate on the meaning of Sullivan should continue, it is undoubtedly time to shake off the unexamined self-satisfaction that frequently accompanies media accounts of this momentous legal drama.

One transformative approach is to continue to celebrate the ***importance*** of ***Sullivan,*** but also to reframe its ***origins.***

The civil rights movement ***set the stage*** for ***Sullivan*** and served as the catalyst for the Supreme Court's historic decision protecting our First Amendment right to freedom of press.
Fred Gray
History should note the ***role*** of the ***civil rights movement*** in enhancing the rights of ***every*** American for generations to come by the legal precepts announced in ***New York Times v. Sullivan.***

Once the ***Sullivan*** decision is understood, Trump's claims about libel law are easily dispensed with as ***inaccurate*** at best.

SHOO!

Contrary to his repeated assertions, the press is ***not at all*** protected from making "totally false and knowingly false" statements.

If the media lies, the actual malice standard does ***not*** shield them from the repercussions of publishing what they know to be ***false,*** and they would undoubtedly ***lose*** a libel suit regarding any such public remarks.

What the Court recognized in ***Sullivan*** is that the First Amendment ***itself*** limits the bounds of state libel law.

Consequently, the free press protections that Trump objects to are ***constitutional*** in nature and ***can't be changed*** by the president or even Congress.

It is not clear whether Trump does not ***understand*** the ***actual malice*** test or is ***intentionally*** misrepresenting the state of the law to make the news media look like they are ***running amok*** without ***standards.***

Whatever the reason, it seemed that ***this*** president was following in the direct footsteps of ***another*** president who also viewed the media as his ***enemy.***

The goddam press can do anything.
Malice is ***impossible,*** virtually. What the hell ***happened?*** What's the name of that— I don't remember the ***case,*** but it was a ***horrible decision.***

President Richard M. Nixon

The ***similarities*** between the Nixon and Trump statements on libel are telling. When presidents feel particularly ***threatened*** by press scrutiny, they ***lash out*** at First Amendment protections.

PRESS

Understanding the history of ***Sullivan*** enables Americans to better understand the ***motivations*** of the president, and any public figure, when they attack libel law and the free press protections that are now a ***constitutionally required*** part of it.

Let's give the ***last word*** in this ongoing debate on constitutional interpretation to ***Justice Thurgood Marshall.*** In a thought-provoking speech he delivered for the bicentennial of the Constitution, Marshall addressed the ***conflict*** inherent between celebrating the Constitution for what it ***was,*** and what it was to ***become.*** As with ***Sullivan, racial justice*** was at the heart of the issue.

I do not believe that the meaning of the Constitution was forever ***"fixed"*** at the Philadelphia Convention. Nor do I find the wisdom, foresight, and sense of justice exhibited by the Framers particularly ***profound.*** To the ***contrary,*** the government they devised was ***defective from the start,*** requiring ***several amendments,*** a ***civil war,*** and ***momentous social transformation*** to attain the system of constitutional government, and its respect for the ***individual freedoms*** and ***human rights,*** we hold as fundamental today.

The
CONStitution

When contemporary Americans cite "The Constitution," they invoke a concept that is ***vastly different*** from what the Framers barely began to construct two centuries ago....

What is striking is the role ***legal principles*** have played throughout America's history in determining the condition of Negroes. They were ***enslaved*** by law, ***emancipated*** by law, ***disenfranchised*** and ***segregated*** by law; and, finally, they have begun to ***win equality*** by law. Along the way, ***new constitutional principles*** have emerged to meet the challenges of a changing society. The progress has been ***dramatic,*** and it ***will continue.***

The men who gathered in Philadelphia in 1787 could not have envisioned these changes. They could not have ***imagined,*** nor would they have accepted, that the document they were drafting would one day be construed by a Supreme Court to which had been appointed a ***woman*** and the descendant of an ***African slave.*** "We the People" no longer enslave, but the credit does not belong to the Framers. It belongs to those who ***refused to acquiesce*** in outdated notions of "liberty," "justice," and "equality," and who strived to better them....

If we seek, instead, a sensitive understanding of the Constitution's inherent ***defects,*** and its promising evolution through two hundred years of history...We will see that the ***true miracle*** was not the ***birth*** of the Constitution, but its ***life...***as a living document.

Chapter 4:
STUDENT SPEECH FROM THE VIETNAM WAR TO THE NATIONAL SCHOOL WALKOUT

On March 14, 2018, at 10 a.m., almost ***1 million students*** across the country ***walked out*** of their classrooms. They were saying ***#Enough*** to gun violence and the ***inability of adults*** in this country to make any significant progress on gun safety.

#MARCH FOR OUR LIVES
MARJORY STONEMAN DOUGLAS
HIGH SCHOOL

Coming just one month after seventeen students and staff members of Marjory Stoneman Douglas High School had been ***shot to death*** in Parkland, Florida, many walkouts included seventeen minutes of silence to honor those victims.

Inspired by the activism of the student survivors from Parkland, the National School Walkout marked the beginning of a student movement to demand action from Congress on gun control legislation.
The Parkland students, some of whom formed the March for Our Lives organization, were determined to disrupt the traditionally brief responses to mass shootings and insist that the issue remain a part of the national conversation.
MARCH FOR OUR LIVES

Notwithstanding the success of these student demonstrations in capturing ***national attention,*** many of those participating were aware that there could be ***consequences*** for making their voices heard.

"We will ***discipline*** no matter if it is one, fifty, or five hundred students involved. ***All*** will be suspended for 3 days and parent notes will not alleviate the discipline," one superintendent in Texas posted on Facebook.

TIME
ENOUGH.
SCHOOL

These student activists were faced with **real uncertainty** about the extent of their First Amendment rights in school and what would happen to them afterward.
Although they did not have to worry about the **violent retribution** that faced civil rights student protesters in the 1960s, their worries were still **real** and **understandable.**
In this time of renewed **student activism,** looking to **history** will not only provide **inspiration** for how students make social progress, but will also provide **answers.** Let's examine a protest during the **Vietnam War** in an unlikely place by three unlikely students, whose efforts would end up forging a **new path** for student speech rights in America.
On December 16, 1965, **Mary Beth Tinker** was a thirteen-year-old student in the eighth grade at Warren Harding Junior High School in Des Moines, Iowa.
As she walked to school that morning, she was **"really nervous"** because she was wearing something that she **knew** was going to get her into **trouble.**
It was a simple **black armband** over her sweater, made from cloth found in her mother's sewing materials. She was wearing it to mourn "the dead in **Vietnam** on both sides of the war" and to support **Senator Robert Kennedy's** "call for a Christmas truce...when there was this **tremendous bombing** of North Vietnam."

Mary Beth had recently attended a meeting of a Unitarian youth group, ***Liberal Religious Youth,*** where some students "decided to wear these black armbands to school."
The group may have chosen armbands as their protest symbol, Mary Beth later recalled, because people wore them at a memorial service for the ***four Black girls*** killed in the 1963 Birmingham church bombing by the Ku Klux Klan, which she and her family had attended in Des Moines.
After the meeting, one of the students who attended wrote an article for his high school newspaper announcing their plans. This quickly led to the school district imposing a ban on armbands in their junior high and high schools. The ***threat of punishment*** made most of the fifty students who had planned to wear armbands ***reconsider.***
Mary Beth, however, did not waver.
Mary Beth wore her armband that morning, and there was no hostility or altercations.
But when she arrived at Mr. Moberly's math class, he was waiting for her by the door with "a ***pink slip*** in his hand." She "knew she was in trouble then," and her "heart was racing" as she reported to the ***principal's office.***

Mary Beth felt intimidated by the school authorities and agreed to take off the armband. Nevertheless, she was suspended and sent home.
PRINCIPAL'S OFFICE

That same morning, Christopher Eckhardt, a fifteen-year-old sophomore, was "fearful and trembling" as he entered Theodore Roosevelt High School. Pinned to his arm was a two-inch-wide piece of black cloth.

Christopher stopped at his locker, and then went directly to the principal's office on his own accord.
He spoke with Vice Principal Donald Blackman, who repeatedly asked him to remove the armband. Christopher refused and asserted that wearing it was his constitutional right.

The guidance counselor joined them and told Christopher that "colleges didn't accept protestors" and that if he was suspended, he should look for another high school to return to afterward.

Blackman then cryptically told him that the "senior boys were not going to like" his actions and asked if he "was looking for a busted nose."

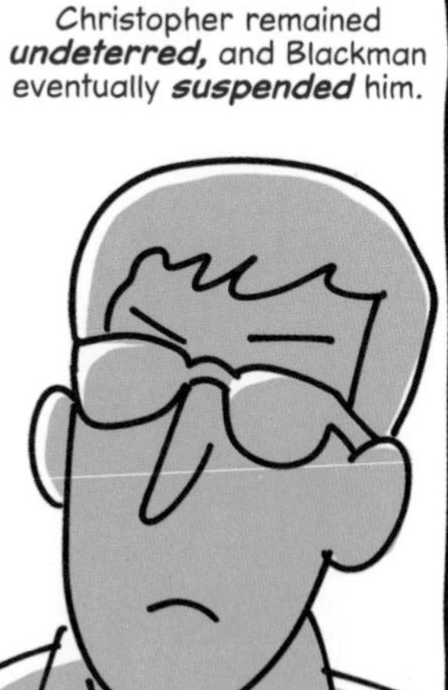
Christopher remained undeterred, and Blackman eventually suspended him.

Mary Beth's older brother, John, who was fifteen and a high school sophomore, decided to wear an armband to school the next day.

By lunchtime he was sent to the principal's office. Principal Donald M. Wetter tried a respectful approach to convince John to take off the armband. Wetter talked about his personal experiences in ***World War II*** and the value of ***patriotism.***

John remembered the principal also telling him that "it was important to ***support our government*** during times of ***war.*** He said that I might have been ***influenced*** by ***Communist propaganda.*** But I told him that I had already thought about what I was doing, and that I was not going to remove the armband. So then he told me that I would have to leave the school and not come back with the armband on."

Two other students were also disciplined for wearing armbands. However, it was only the ***Tinker*** and ***Eckhardt*** families who wanted to pursue the issue. They sought out the help of the ***Iowa Civil Liberties Union*** (ICLU), who represented the students at two ***contentious*** public meetings of the local school board.
ICLU

Ultimately, the board members voted 5 to 2 to uphold the ban on armbands.

On the advice of their counsel, Mary Beth, John, and Christopher returned to school after New Year's Day and did not wear armbands. Instead, they wore ***black clothes*** to class for the rest of the school year, to continue making a statement. "It was our way of fighting back," Mary Beth explained.

With the financial support of the ICLU, ***Dan Johnston*** was hired to bring the case to federal court. Johnston was only twenty-eight years old and "one year out of law school," when he prepared to file a lawsuit seeking a court order to rescind the ban on armbands.

Since their protests had become public, the Tinkers and Eckhardts had withstood ***menacing phone calls*** and ***notes*** that threatened to ***bomb*** them, ***shoot*** them, or suggested they should "go back to Russia if you like Communism so much."

The ***anger*** directed toward the young protesters and their families must be considered (though not justified) in the context of the national attitude toward the Vietnam War at the time. In 1965, most Americans still strongly ***supported*** the war, and dissenting views were far from mainstream.

One Gallup poll in 1965 found ***60%*** of Americans believed that sending U.S. troops to Vietnam was ***"not a mistake,"*** as opposed to only ***24%*** who answered that it was.

Another element likely fueling the rage against these youthful dissenters was that student protest was still considered a radical new cultural development.
Despite the fact that it was teenage students who launched the lunch-counter sit-ins that became such a successful part of the civil rights movement, many adults remained highly skeptical of student activism.

In her book, historian ***Kathryn Schumaker*** captures how "the increased involvement of young people in social movements" was met with ***condemnation*** and ***scorn*** in the 1960s:
KATHRYN SCHUMAKER
TROUBLEMAKERS
STUDENTS' RIGHTS AND RACIAL JUSTICE IN THE LONG 1960S
That high school students had the right to be heard was patently absurd to many and deeply disturbing to others who worried that the disruptions of the era jeopardized the ability of schools to carry out their mission to educate all young people. Their claims were frivolous, their methods crude, and their efforts the result of youthful immaturity. Why should anyone care what teenagers think?

On September 1, 1966, ***Chief Judge Roy Stephenson,*** in the District Court for the Southern District of Iowa, ruled ***in favor*** of the school district. He acknowledged that wearing the armbands ***did*** constitute a "***symbolic act***" that was ***protected speech*** under the ***First Amendment.***

However, Stephenson concluded that the armband prohibition was "reasonable" and therefore ruled that it was "the ***disciplined atmosphere*** of the classroom, not the plaintiffs' ***right*** to wear armbands on school premises, which is entitled to the protection of the law."

On appeal, the case was argued before all eight judges of the Eighth Circuit, who split ***evenly,*** 4 to 4, and issued a one-paragraph order ***affirming*** the lower court's decision. Now the students had only one last unlikely remaining chance: the ***United States Supreme Court.***

FREEDOM
NOW
CORE
ONE MAN
SNCC
ONE VOTE

There was one glimmer of hope in their effort to be granted a hearing by the Supreme Court, and it came from ***other*** student protesters.

More than a ***year*** before the Tinkers and Eckhardt wore their armbands, ***Black*** students at the segregated Booker T. Washington High School in Philadelphia, Mississippi, were wearing a different kind of protest symbol: ***freedom buttons.*** This was the same town where, only months earlier, three civil rights activists, ***James Chaney, Andrew Goodman,*** and ***Mickey Schwerner,*** were ***murdered*** by members of the local Ku Klux Klan.

As many as ***forty students*** wore the buttons, and the majority of them chose to be sent home when their principal told them that regulations required them to remove the pins or be suspended. In the case that would be called ***Burnside v. Byars,*** the Fifth Circuit determined that wearing the buttons would ***not*** "inherently distract students," and that school officials ***could not*** "infringe on their students' right to free and unrestricted expression... where the exercise of such rights...do not materially and substantially interfere with the requirements of appropriate discipline in the operation of the school."

Burnside
v.
Byars

The **Burnside** decision meant that **two** circuit courts had considered very **similar** cases on the rights of students to symbolically express dissent in their schools, and come to seemingly **opposite** legal conclusions.
This circuit split made **Tinker** even more **ripe for review** by the Supreme Court. Sure enough, the armband students would soon hear their silent protests argued **aloud** before the justices of the high court.

In the almost ***three years*** between the armband protests in Des Moines and the Supreme Court oral argument for the Tinker case in D.C., much had changed in the country. ***Martin Luther King Jr.*** and ***Robert F. Kennedy*** had been ***assassinated.***

More than ***30,000 Americans*** had ***died*** in Vietnam during this period. ***Public opinion*** had continued to ***shift*** such that Americans had become ***equally divided*** on the Vietnam War.

Anti-war protests were sweeping college campuses. At Columbia University in 1968, almost a ***thousand students,*** protesting the war and the school's treatment of its Black neighbors in Harlem, took over five buildings on campus. The standoff lasted a week and ended with more than ***700 arrested*** in violent confrontations with the police. ***Black armbands*** were beginning to look more ***quaint*** than radical. Expressions of student dissent could now be seen as part of a youth revolt.

Amid this national turmoil, Dan Johnston was about to argue his first case before the United States Supreme Court. The leading case supporting Johnston's advocacy for the First Amendment was ***Barnette,*** which established that students couldn't be compelled to speak a message that went ***against*** their beliefs.

Dan Johnston
However, as constitutional law professor Justin Driver deftly explains:
Barnette did not establish that students possessed an affirmative right to advance their own opinions, on topics of their own selection, much less in the face of school officials' objections. The right to sit out, in other words, did not necessarily confer the right to speak out.
Professor Justin Driver

Justice Byron White began to grill Johnston with a series of questions about the distraction the armbands could cause.

Don't you think it would cause some people to direct their attention to the armband and the Vietnam War and think about that rather than what they were...supposed to be thinking about in the classroom?

Johnston had to concede the armbands "might for a few moments" take students' minds off their work, but attempted to counter that it would do so no more than other distractions that were allowed in the classroom.

What if the regulation had been expanded to limit armbands or buttons or placards? Would that have made a difference?
FREEDOM NOW CORE
Justice Byron White

Would expressive rights go so far as to include a child wearing an outlandish costume because they wanted to express a very strong belief in the utmost freedom for the individual?
Justice Abe Fortas

I worry that such line drawing would get the Supreme Court pretty deep in the trenches of ordinary day-to-day school district business.
Chief Justice Earl Warren

I really would not think it would get you any further in that sort of thing than in Barnette... Whatever are the delicate functions of school boards... they still have no function that cannot be exercised within the purview and within the dictates of this Court's decision under the First Amendment.
Dan Johnston

Arguing on behalf of the school district was their longtime counsel, ***Allan Herrick.*** In contrast to the youthful and inexperienced Johnston, Herrick was in his late sixties, a law firm partner, WWI veteran, and a conservative Republican. A classic establishment figure right out of central casting, Herrick had been described as being infuriated by the anti-war protests.

PROTEST

Herrick started off ***strong.*** The school board's position was that administrators should not "have to wait until ***violence, disorder*** and ***disruption*** break out," but rather should be able to restrict speech when "in their ***reasonable discretion*** and ***judgment,*** disorder and disruption of the scholarly atmosphere of the school will result unless they act ***firmly*** and ***promptly."*** Resorting to an effective ***cliché,*** Herrick reminded the court that "sometimes an ounce of ***prevention*** is a lot better than a pound of ***cure."***

Do we have anything more than your ***assertion*** that they used due care and they were ***reasonable?"***
Justice Thurgood Marshall

Herrick claimed the board's actions were indeed ***reasonable*** because of "the ***explosive situation*** that existed in the Des Moines schools at the time." Marshall then wanted to know exactly ***what*** made the situation so explosive.

TNT

A former student of one of our high schools was killed in Vietnam. Some of his friends are still in the school. It was felt that if any kind of a demonstration existed, it might evolve into something which would be difficult to control.
Do we have a city in this country that hasn't had someone killed in Vietnam?
No, I think not, Your Honor. But I don't think it would be an explosive situation in most cases. But if someone is going to appear...with an armband...protesting the thing, that it could be explosive...
It could be. Is that your position?
Yes, sir. It could be.
And there was no evidence that it would be? Is that the rule you want us to adopt?
No, not at all, Your Honor.

Herrick was *floundering.* It was an unusually terrible performance before the highest court in the land. Herrick was simply *unable* to provide any factual basis to support his inflammatory rhetoric, and his time ran out without him being able to improve his situation.

On rebuttal, Johnston emphasized that there was "no general prohibition against political emblems" and that "other kinds of political insignia including the Iron Cross were worn in the schools." His implied point was that the school district only cared about restricting political symbols that expressed a message that they disagreed with.
As the clock was running out on Johnston, Justice Black fired off a final accusatory question:

Which do you think has the most right about control in the school...the pupils or the authorities that are running the school?

The authorities that are running the schools...
under the authority given [to] them by the Constitution of the United States and within the provisions of that Constitution. And the whole nub of our case is that... they've exceeded their powers under that.

In the end, the novice lawyer felt optimistic about their chances. As they walked out together, Christopher Eckhardt remembered Johnston being "high as a kite on the job he did" and that they all felt "exhilarated."

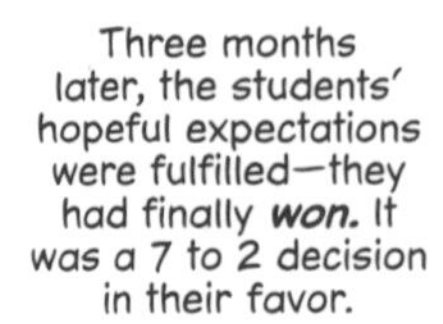
Three months later, the students' hopeful expectations were fulfilled—they had finally **won.** It was a 7 to 2 decision in their favor.

Justice Abe Fortas wrote for the majority in a rousing style that reads more like a political ***essay*** than a typical Supreme Court opinion.

"It can hardly be argued that either students or teachers ***shed*** their ***constitutional rights*** to ***freedom*** of ***speech*** or ***expression*** at the ***schoolhouse gate.***"

Justice Fortas

SCHOOL
No matter whatever else ***Tinker*** would mean in the future, it would forever be credited with bringing about this ***memorable phrasing*** that for the ***first time*** recognized ***student speech*** as having constitutional value ***equal*** to that of adults.

"In our system, undifferentiated fear or apprehension of ***disturbance*** is not enough to overcome the ***right*** to freedom of expression. Any departure from absolute regimentation may cause ***trouble.***
"Any variation from the majority's opinion may inspire ***fear.*** Any word spoken, in class, in the lunch room, or on the campus, that deviates from the views of another person may start an argument or cause a ***disturbance.***
"But our ***Constitution*** says we ***must*** take this risk, and our history says that it is this sort of ***hazardous freedom***—this kind of ***openness***—that is the basis of our ***national strength*** and of the independence and vigor of Americans who grow up and live in this relatively ***permissive,*** often ***disputatious,*** society."
RISK

Fortas did, however, acknowledge that schools needed to have the power to ***limit*** or ***prohibit*** student speech or expression in ***certain circumstances.***

HALT!

The test Fortas set forth, taken directly from the ***Burnside*** case, required school authorities to ***"reasonably...forecast substantial disruption*** of or material interference with school activities," or with "the rights of others" in order to restrict student speech in advance.

In other words, in order to ***restrict*** student speech, school officials must be able to reasonably point to something ***more*** than ***unsubstantiated fear,*** and the disruption they predict must be ***substantial.***

Justice Fortas wrapped up his opinion by contrasting the ***limits*** on schools, with the ***freedoms*** of students:

"State-operated schools may not be enclaves of ***totalitarianism.*** School officials do not possess absolute authority over their students. Students in school, as well as out of school, are ***'persons'*** under our Constitution.

"They are possessed of fundamental ***rights*** which the State must respect. Students may not be regarded as ***closed-circuit recipients*** of only that which the State chooses to communicate. They may not be ***confined*** to the expression of those sentiments that are officially approved.

"In the absence of a specific showing of ***constitutionally valid*** reasons to regulate their speech, students are ***entitled*** to ***freedom of expression*** of their views."

The decision remains a tribute to the ***power*** of protest, and these three teenagers' ability to transform two inches of ***black cloth*** into a force that would ***revolutionize*** student speech rights.

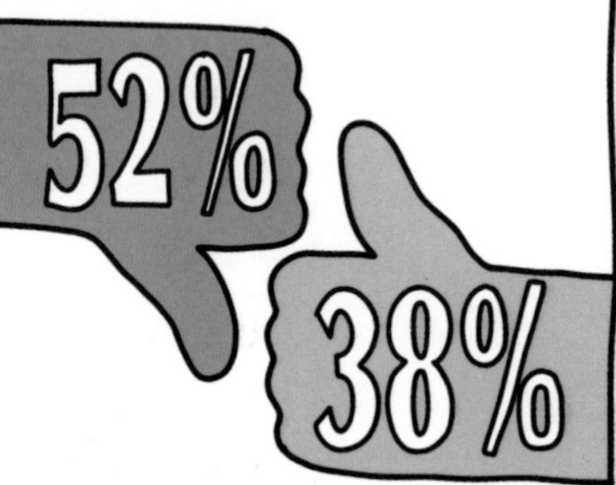
One month after the decision, 52% of those surveyed did *not* believe that students had a right to protest, as opposed to just 38% supporting such rights.
52%
38%

Tinker would prove to be the high-water mark for student speech rights. In three subsequent cases from the 1980s to 2007, the Supreme Court granted school officials ***greater authority*** to ***restrict*** student expression in specific contexts.
• ***Bethel School District v. Fraser***
• ***Hazelwood School District v. Kuhlmeier***
• ***Morse v. Frederick***

Schools can now control student speech that is ***"vulgar and lewd"...***

..."school-sponsored"...
School Gazette

...and ***"promoting illegal drug use."***

THE
PUBLIC EDUCATION,
SCHOOL-
THE SUPREME COURT,
HOUSE
AND THE BATTLE FOR
GATE
THE AMERICAN MIND
JUSTIN DRIVER
Nevertheless, Professor ***Justin Driver*** persuasively contends that these decisions...
...did not purport to undercut ***Tinker's*** core contribution: students, typically speaking, continue to possess the right to express themselves in schools, even if educators do not support their messages.
Professor Justin Driver

What lessons then do ***Tinker*** and its progeny hold for the participants in the ***National Student Walkout, March for Our Lives,*** and millions of ***other*** students considering protesting ***at*** their schools about gun violence ***in*** their schools?

#MARCH FOR OUR LIVES

At its most ***fundamental*** level, ***Tinker*** means that students can wear armbands, or buttons, to protest gun violence, draw attention to gun safety laws, and mourn the dead, as long as it wouldn't reasonably lead to a substantial disruption in school.

ONE MAN
SNCC
ONE VOTE

And thanks to ***Tinker,*** this should be true no matter how ***unpopular*** or ***controversial*** the message is in some communities or with school administrators. Of course, students also have an equal right to wear pro-Second Amendment messages as well.

Yet ***walking out of class*** during the school day, for any reason, is a ***different story.*** This type of ***disruptive activity*** would not be protected by ***Tinker.***

Schools can typically discipline students for ***missing*** class, even if they're doing so to participate in a protest or otherwise express themselves. But what the school ***can't*** do is discipline students ***more harshly*** because they are walking out to express a political view or because school administrators don't support the views behind the protest.

ACLU

Given the ***savvy*** and ***sophistication*** on the part of the Parkland students so far, it seems likely that they have known about their First Amendment rights for some time.

TIME
ENOUGH.

The ***effectiveness*** of these poised, articulate, well-informed, and seemingly preternaturally mature student leaders of Stoneman Douglas [was in large part due to their excellent ***public school*** that] painstakingly taught about drama, media, free speech, political activism, and forensics.
Slate's legal correspondent ***Dahlia Lithwick***

Another meaningful learning opportunity that Marjory Stoneman Douglas High School gave to their students was to provide a forum for ***Mary Beth Tinker*** to speak with their class in 2013.

Tinker's message, then and now, about how student protest ***can make a difference,*** should certainly be one that resonates with many of the Parkland students today as they seek to make ***change*** in their schools and across the country.

I was really excited that they were taking their ***grief*** and turning it into something positive... I do believe we're at a ***turning point,*** for not only gun violence but for young people having more of a say over the policies that affect their lives.

In 1968, only six months before hearing oral argument in the ***Tinker*** case, Justice Abe Fortas had a highly unusual book published, entitled *Concerning Dissent and Civil Disobedience,* which sought to explain "the basic principles governing dissent and ***civil disobedience*** in our democracy."

Abe Fortas
ASSOCIATE JUSTICE
SUPREME COURT OF THE UNITED STATES
CONCERNING DISSENT AND CIVIL DISOBEDIENCE
"WE HAVE AN ALTERNATIVE TO VIOLENCE"
"ONE OF THE MOST VALUABLE BOOKS OF THE YEAR" -THE NEW YORK TIMES
750,000 COPIES IN PRINT

In one passage, the man who would become the author of the ***greatest decision*** for students' rights offers sage commentary that manages to speak with ***equal force*** to the Vietnam War protesters of the ***past*** and the March for Our Lives movement of ***today...***

"I do not know how profound in intensity or how lasting the current youth revolt may be. It may presage a new and welcome era of idealism in the nation.

"It may forecast the development of ***greater maturity*** and independence of outlook among our young people, and this may be productive of ***much good.***

"In any event, it presents a ***challenge*** to the ***older generations*** as well as to ***youth*** to reconsider the ***goals*** of our society and its ***values,*** and urgently to reappraise the distribution of ***function*** and ***responsibility*** among the generations."

MARCH FOR OUR LIVES

Chapter 5:

STORMY DANIELS, PRIOR RESTRAINTS, AND THE PENTAGON PAPERS

When a photo of *Stormy Daniels* posing with *Anderson Cooper* was tweeted out by her lawyer with a simple reference to *@60Minutes,* it triggered the *desired effect.*
The media went into a *frenzy* of speculation about what the adult-film star would *say* now that she appeared ready to talk about her alleged affair with *Donald Trump.*

THE WALL STREET JOURNAL

It had been almost two months since *The Wall Street Journal* broke the story that Trump's personal lawyer, ***Michael Cohen,*** just ***days*** before the presidential election, had arranged a ***$130,000 payment*** to Daniels for signing a ***nondisclosure agreement.*** It seemed she was ready to ***break the terms*** of that agreement. If you want to speak out and be taken seriously, *60 Minutes* would be the ideal place to tell your story.

MICHAEL COHEN
PAY TO: STORMY DANIELS
AMOUNT: ONE HUNDRED & THIRTY THOUSAND DOLLARS

However, just a few days after the announcement, the conversation began to turn from ***when*** the interview would air to questions about ***if*** it would air at all.

STOP

A growing chorus of media outlets were soon reporting that Trump's ***legal team*** might seek a ***court order*** to stop *60 Minutes* from televising the interview.

CBS News President ***David Rhodes***
It has been reported there will be an ***injunction*** to prevent it from running. I haven't seen such an injunction, and I don't know what the ***basis*** of such an injunction would be.

Rhodes was understandably at a loss to think of a sufficient legal argument to support this restriction on the press.

His ***confidence*** stemmed from what has become known as the ***Pentagon Papers*** case, which struck a decisive blow against ***censorship of the press,*** even when the reporting was on ***top secret*** military intelligence during wartime. Although the official case name was ***New York Times Company v. United States,*** the real antagonists were ***President Nixon*** versus a ***free press.***

Today we take for granted the right of the press to publish material received from leakers and others who provide it in violation of the law.
However, in 1971, the outcome of this fight was very much in doubt and set the stage for the most thrilling conflict in First Amendment history.
The stakes could not have been higher. The Supreme Court review occurred in record time (fifteen days) and the result likely flipped on a single answer at oral argument.

What would later become known as the Pentagon Papers began as a study commissioned in 1967 by an increasingly disillusioned Defense Secretary Robert McNamara.
McNamara's instructions were that the report be "encyclopedic and objective." He got his wish. A year and a half later the completed study was presented to a new defense secretary, all forty-seven volumes and 7,000 pages, composed of 3,000 pages of narrative and 4,000 pages of supporting documents.
It was classified top secret, the military's highest level of national security information classification, which applies only to secrets that, if revealed, "could result in exceptionally grave damage to the nation."
The government continued to consider the report so secret that it was not fully declassified until 2011.
History of U.S. Decision-Making in Vietnam, 1945-68
Defense Secretary Robert McNamara
SECRET
TOP SECRET
TOP SECRET

Daniel Ellsberg, the man responsible for ***releasing*** the *Pentagon Papers,* would later describe the documents as revealing "a policy of ***concealment*** and quite ***deliberate deception*** from the Truman administration onward" about America's role in Vietnam.

Daniel Ellsberg

Of more immediate interest to the country, the report showed the ***bombing*** taking place in ***North Vietnam*** was ***not*** deterring Viet Cong fighters and wasn't working to bring an end to the seemingly ***endless war.***

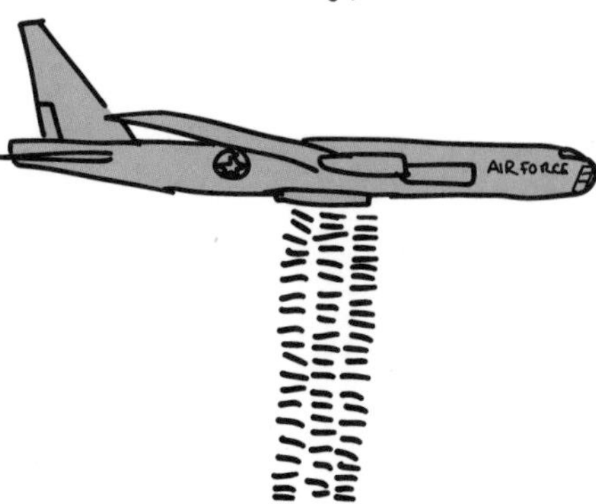
AIR FORCE

Floyd Abrams, the lawyer who would defend *The New York Times* in the *Pentagon Papers* case, put it simply:

The documents were ***devastating,*** demonstrating an extraordinary level of governmental duplicity based upon an unprecedented source—the very files of the ***Government itself.***

Who ***was*** Ellsberg, the man who was both a contributing ***author*** of and then ***leaked*** the *Pentagon Papers*? Dubbed ***"the most dangerous man in America"*** by then Secretary of State ***Henry Kissinger,*** he was perhaps one of the most unlikely radicals in American history.

A Harvard-educated economist and former marine commander, Ellsberg volunteered to serve in Vietnam as a "State Department civilian." After two years, Ellsberg became convinced that "continuing the hopeless war [was] ***intolerable.***" He still remained a consummate insider who acted as an adviser on the war to presidential candidates and ***Henry Kissinger*** in his role as national security adviser.

In 1969, he attended an ***anti-war conference*** and heard a speech by an activist who talked about his plans to go to jail to ***resist the draft.*** He surprised himself, he later recalled, by ***breaking down*** and ***sobbing*** for more than an hour, thinking "we are eating our young."

Ellsberg began ***secretly*** removing portions of one of the copies of the *Pentagon Papers* to photocopy page by page. He brought the papers to anti-war senators, but they ***refused*** to make the documents ***public.***

Feeling increasingly ***desperate*** that the papers would never be released, Ellsberg took the riskier step of giving access to ***Neil Sheehan,*** a respected Vietnam reporter with *The New York Times.*

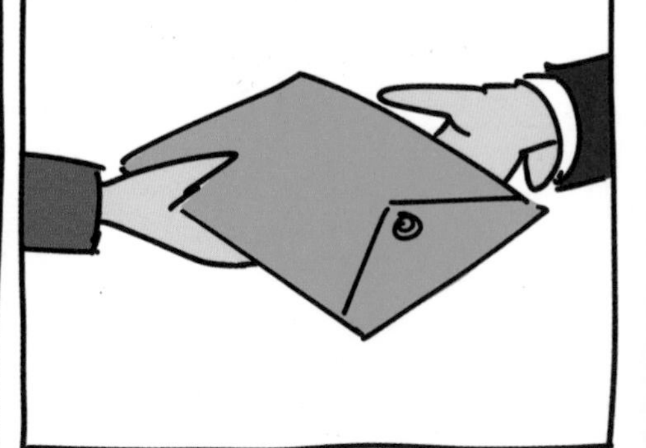

A team from *The New York Times* soon decamped with the papers to a secret hotel suite and began a voracious ***three-month*** review. They would later describe their efforts as a race to absorb the information, corroborate its accuracy, and determine what could be reported on without potentially compromising ***national security.*** Meanwhile, the editors, lawyers, and publisher of the *The New York Times* began a fierce internal ***debate*** as to whether to publish or report on the *Pentagon Papers* at all.

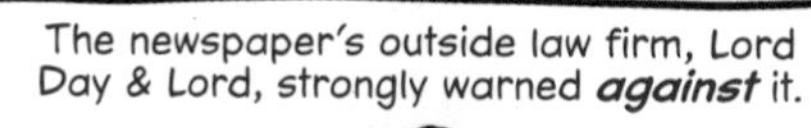

The newspaper's outside law firm, Lord Day & Lord, strongly warned ***against*** it.

The publisher, Arthur O. Sulzberger, was advised that publication of the top secret documents would violate the ***Espionage Act*** and that he could be jailed himself.

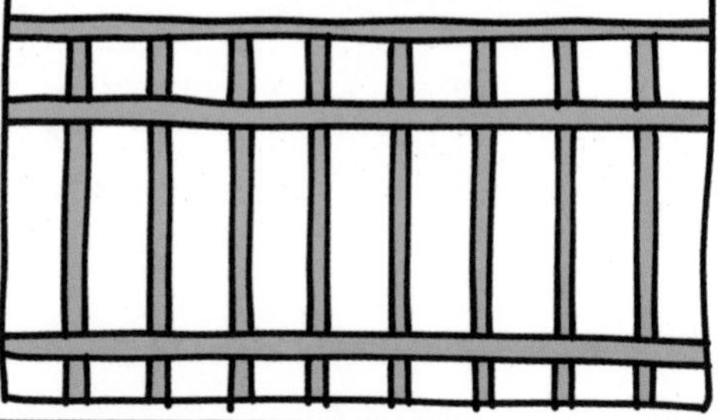

Undeterred, on ***Sunday, June 13, 1971,*** *The New York Times* published its first article on the *Pentagon Papers*, with the uninvitingly dry headline:

The New York Times

NEW YORK, SUNDAY, JUNE 13, 1971

Vietnam Archive: Pentagon Study Traces 3 Decades of Growing U. S. Involvement

BY NEIL SHEEHAN

CITY TO DISCLOSE BUDGETARY TRIMS

s Vows
e House

Three pages of documents from the study were published verbatim inside the paper, but an average reader's attention might have been drawn to a more prominent front-page article...
Initially Nixon did not appear very **concerned** about the publication since he was advised it would mostly reflect badly on the ***Democrats.***

Tricia Nixon Takes Vows
In Garden at White House

But during a phone call with ***Henry Kissinger...***
This is ***treasonable action*** on the part of the bastards that put it out!
President Richard M. Nixon
There's ***no question*** it's actionable. I'm absolutely ***certain*** that this violates all sorts of ***security laws.***
Henry Kissinger

By the end of the call, they agreed to have Attorney *General* ***John Mitchell*** examine options on how to respond.

The ***next day,*** after *The New York Times* published its ***second*** front-page article on the *Pentagon Papers,* Mitchell told Nixon that they would look "a little foolish" not to take action against the newspaper.

e New York Tim

NEW YORK, MONDAY, JUNE 14, 1971

Vietnam Archive: A Consensus to Bomb Developed Before '64 Election, Study Says

By NEIL SHEEHAN

In a fateful and extremely brief exchange, Nixon asked a pivotal question:
Has this ever been done before?
A *publication* like this, or—
No, no, no. Have you—has the *government* ever done this to a *paper* before?
Oh, *yes,* advising them of their...
Oh.
Yes, we've done this before.
Have we? All right.
Mitchell's answer was shockingly ***misleading.*** In fact, the federal government had ***never before*** in American history brought an action to stop a newspaper from publishing.

Perhaps bolstered by this ***false precedent,*** Nixon had made up his mind.
As far as the *Times* is concerned, hell, they're our ***enemies.*** I think we just ought to do it.

Mitchell sent a telegram to ***Sulzberger,*** stating that continued publication of the *Pentagon Papers* "will cause ***irreparable injury*** to the defense interests of the United States," and requested that the newspaper ***stop*** publishing the information and ***return the documents*** to the Defense Department.

The *Times* refused, and published an article the next morning with a blaring all-caps headline:

MITCHELL SEEKS TO HALT SERIES ON VIETNAM BUT TIMES REFUSES

Underneath this declaration of independence was a ***third*** article on the *Pentagon Papers* and how President Lyndon B. Johnson had "secretly opened [the] way to ground combat."

The Civil Division of the United States Attorney's Office in Manhattan sought an ***emergency order*** to prevent the *Times* from publishing another word of the *Pentagon Papers.*
Meanwhile, the *Times* was unceremoniously ***dumped*** by the law firm that had represented the newspaper for more than sixty years. This was an unmistakable sign of how ***radically*** their decision to continue publishing was perceived in some legal circles.
STOP

Fortuitously, the general counsel for the *Times* had made a middle-of-the-night call to hire Yale constitutional law professor ***Alexander Bickel*** and up-and-coming First Amendment attorney ***Floyd Abrams,*** who eagerly took on the case and confidently told the *New York Times* leadership that it "would obviously ***win.***"

Alexander Bickel
Floyd Abrams

Abrams later recalled that his initial exuberance ***diminished*** as he realized that his case was about to be "litigated by an academic with ***no courtroom experience,*** accompanied by a lawyer who had ***never*** even ***watched*** a Supreme Court argument."

The request for an injunction had been assigned to ***Judge Murray Gurfein,*** a Nixon appointee with a ***"dazzling intellect,"*** who was so new to the bench, this would be his ***very first case.***

The New York Times made the risky but principled decision to refuse the judge's request to voluntarily stop publishing during his legal review. As a result, Gurfein granted the government's demand for a temporary restraining order, barring the Times from publishing anything further on the Pentagon Papers.
The Times then had to make another fateful decision: whether to obey the judge's order.
Professor Bickel convinced Sulzberger that they must follow the court's order and not publish for the time being.
His prevailing argument was that the newspaper could not violate the rule of law to vindicate the rule of law.
In other words, to prove that their act of publishing top secret documents was lawful, they must follow and abide by the legal process. The series stopped.
Bickel and Abrams had two primary arguments to convince the judge that a permanent order to halt publication must not be granted. First, they made clear that what the government was seeking was a prior restraint—
—a government action (by statute or court order) preventing speech before it occurs—and that the Supreme Court had "consistently rejected all manner of prior restraints on publication" for more than 150 years.
NEWS PAPER

In addition, they took **a broader view** that publication of government documents **exposing** presidential misconduct in war was exactly the type of **press action** that the First Amendment was created to safeguard.
TOP SECRET
In a surprising turn of events, just **three days after** Judge Gurfein had granted the temporary injunction, he ruled that he was **denying** the government's request to stop publication. He found that the government had **failed** to produce enough facts to demonstrate a "sharp clash...between the vital **security interests** of the Nation and the compelling constitutional doctrine against prior restraint."
U-TURN
If there be some **embarrassment** to the Government...that flows from any **security breach,** we must learn to live with it. The security of the Nation is **not** at the ramparts **alone.** Security also lies in the **value of our free institutions.**
NEWS
A **cantankerous press,** an **obstinate press,** a **ubiquitous press** must be suffered by those in authority in order to preserve the even greater values of freedom of expression and the right of the people **to know.** These are troubled times. There is no greater **safety valve** for discontent and cynicism about the affairs of Government than **freedom of expression** in any form. This has been the **genius** of our institutions throughout our history.

It was a resounding ***victory*** from a surprising source. Nonetheless, the judge did maintain the temporary stay on publication while the government appealed his decision.

STOP
(FOR NOW...)

Meanwhile, with any future publication of the *Pentagon Papers* by *The New York Times* in limbo, Ellsberg gave ***another*** copy of the secret documents to *The Washington Post.*

The New York Times

The same day the *Post* published their ***own*** front-page *Pentagon Papers* article, the assistant attorney general (and future Supreme Court chief justice) ***William Rehnquist*** asked the paper's executive editor, ***Ben Bradlee,*** to cease publication.

Ben Bradlee
William Rehnquist

Bradlee ***refused,*** and the attorney general's office hauled them into court the same night, launching a new front in the government's litigation war.

Eventually Ellsberg gave copies of the papers to ***nineteen newspapers,*** and as the government tried to stop four of the publications, one exasperated judge declared they were "asking us to ride herd on a swarm of bees."

PRESS
PRESS

The separate District Court wins for The New York Times and The Washington Post were both appealed and sent back to the District Court for further hearings. The Times chose to appeal directly to the United States Supreme Court which agreed to hear the case, scheduling oral argument for June 26.
Solicitor General Erwin Griswold, representing the United States, arrived with three boxes holding a rare copy of the complete Pentagon Papers. He asserted that the Times and the Post had obtained the Pentagon Papers as part of a "breach of trust."
They know that this material is not theirs, they do not own it... The heart of our case is that [this] publication... will...materially affect the security of the United States. It will affect lives, it will affect the process of determination of the war. It will affect the process of recovering prisoners of war.
He argued that the standard for stopping publication should not be that to continue would result in immediate harm to the United States, but rather irreparable harm. Griswold concluded that "to say that [publication] can only be enjoined if there will be a war tomorrow morning when there is a war now going on is much too narrow."
Erwin Griswold
VIETNAM
NORTH
SOUTH

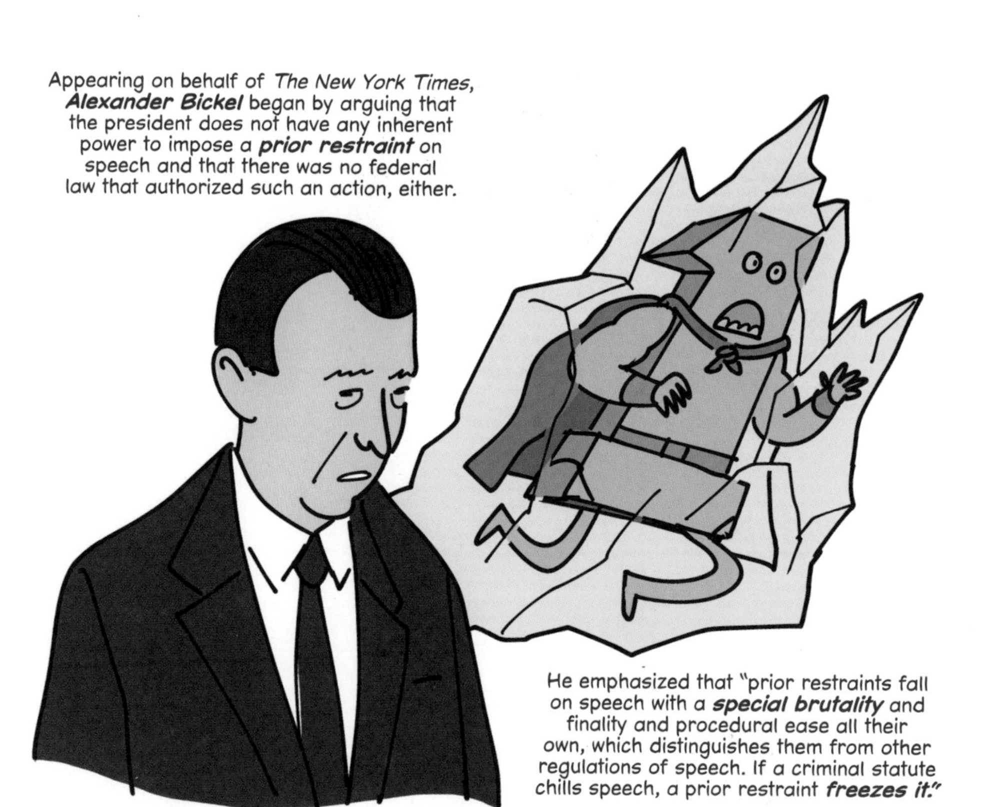
Appearing on behalf of *The New York Times*, **Alexander Bickel** began by arguing that the president does not have any inherent power to impose a ***prior restraint*** on speech and that there was no federal law that authorized such an action, either.
He emphasized that "prior restraints fall on speech with a ***special brutality*** and finality and procedural ease all their own, which distinguishes them from other regulations of speech. If a criminal statute chills speech, a prior restraint ***freezes it.***"

Justice Potter Stewart sprung a potentially ***devastating hypothetical*** on Bickel. What should the Court do if the continued publication of the *Pentagon Papers* would directly and immediately cause the ***deaths*** of one hundred American soldiers?

Try as Bickel might to ***dodge*** the question by maintaining there was ***no evidence*** to support such definite and direct harm in this case, Stewart ***insisted*** on an answer.
You would say the Constitution ***requires*** that it be published and that these men ***die,*** is that it?

No...
I'm afraid I have—I'm afraid my—the inclinations of humanity overcome the somewhat more abstract devotion to the First Amendment in a case of that sort.

The answer seemed to ***surprise*** Justice Stewart, and indeed some of the newspapers' most ardent supporters were also taken aback, viewing it as a ***misguided concession*** on the limits of First Amendment protections. The ACLU even took the highly unusual step of filing a post-oral argument brief ***disavowing*** Bickel's position. And ***Justice Black*** reportedly said in chambers, "Too bad *The New York Times* couldn't find someone who ***believes*** in the First Amendment."

ACLU

In retrospect, however, it seems to have been an astute split-second decision to win over a crucial vote. Sometimes to claim a groundbreaking victory you need to set limits on the extent of what you are asking for, if for no other reason than to highlight the reasonableness of your request.

A whirlwind four days later, the Supreme Court held in a ***6 to 3 decision*** that the government had not met the "heavy burden of showing justification for the imposition" of the prior restraint against the press. The divided Court also held that the injunctions against the newspapers were ***lifted.***

The next day, *The New York Times* resumed its series—which had been halted for fifteen days.

The New York Times

NEW YORK, THURSDAY, JULY 1, 1971

SUPREME COURT, 6-3, UPHOLDS NEWSPAPERS ON PUBLICATION OF THE PENTAGON REPORT; TIMES RESUMES ITS SERIES, HALTED 15 DAYS

Pentagon Papers: Study Reports Kennedy Made 'Gamble' Into a 'Broad Commitment'

BURGER DISSENTS

The triumphant ruling for the press was not as ***sweeping*** as it first appeared. ***Three justices*** issued stinging ***dissenting opinions.***
The dissenters all agreed that ***further hearings*** were warranted in order to give the government more time to prove that ***national security interests*** necessitated overcoming the heavy presumption against prior restraints.
Chief Justice Warren E. Burger
Justice Marshall Harlan II
Justice Harry Blackmun

Even among the majority, no one justice's opinion was supported by more than two justices. This meant that, although six justices voted to allow the newspapers to resume publishing the classified papers, their ***reasons*** for this decision ***differed strikingly.***

Justice Black's opinion, joined by ***Justice Douglas,*** took a free speech ***absolutist*** approach, writing that "every moment's continuance of the injunctions against these newspapers amounts to a flagrant, indefensible, and continuing ***violation*** of the First Amendment." He then set forth on a soaring ***tribute*** to the role of a free press.
Justice Hugo Black
Justice William O. Douglas

In the First Amendment, the Founding Fathers gave the free press the protection it must have to fulfill its ***essential role*** in our democracy. The press was to serve the governed, ***not*** the governors.

NEWS

"The Government's power to censor the press was ***abolished*** so that the press would remain ***forever free*** to censure the Government. The press was ***protected*** so that it could ***bare the secrets*** of government and inform the people.

NEWS

"Only a ***free*** and ***unrestrained*** press can effectively ***expose deception*** in government. And ***paramount*** among the responsibilities of a free press is the ***duty*** to prevent any part of the government from deceiving the people and sending them off to distant lands to ***die*** of foreign fevers and foreign shot and shell.

"In my view, far from deserving ***condemnation*** for their courageous reporting, *The New York Times, The Washington Post*, and other newspapers should be ***commended*** for serving the purpose that the Founding Fathers saw so clearly.

NEWS

"In revealing the workings of government that led to the Vietnam War, the newspapers nobly did precisely that which the Founders ***hoped and trusted*** they would do."

NEWS

Justice Stewart and ***Justice White*** were the swing votes that ultimately turned in favor of the *Times*. Yet Justice Stewart's opinion (joined by Justice White) took a much less ***celebratory*** approach than Justice Black's.

Justice Potter Stewart
Justice Byron White

Stewart stated that he agreed with the government that at least ***some*** of the documents ***should not*** be published in the interest of national security. Nevertheless, sounding almost reluctant, Justice Stewart found that he could not say that publication would ***"surely result in direct, immediate, and irreparable damage to our Nation or its people."***

This phrase would later be understood as establishing the ***key legal test*** to come out of the *Pentagon Papers* case.

It seems Bickel's ***bold concession*** that direct loss of life could trump the First Amendment, not only garnered him the votes needed to win, but contributed to the formation of a test that provided extraordinary—if not absolute—protection of the press.

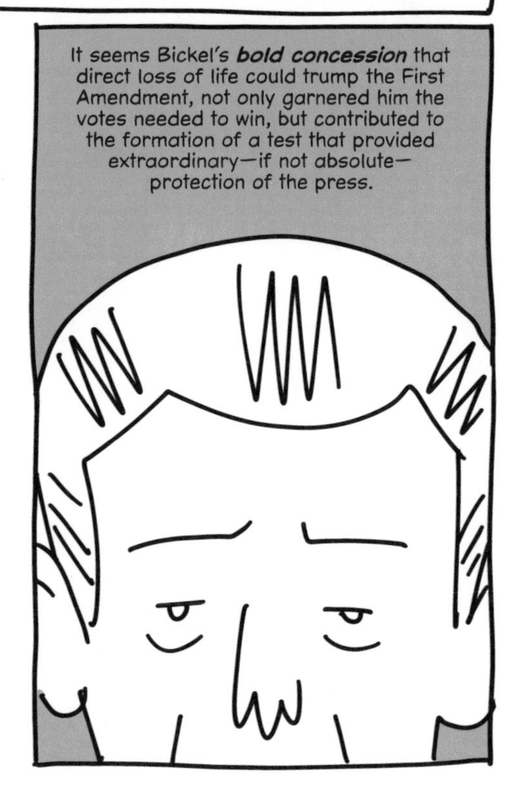

But there was a ***catch.*** A majority of justices indicated that the leakers themselves could still be ***criminally prosecuted.*** The First Amendment shield against prior restraints on ***the press*** would provide no such protection for the man who provided the top secret documents to the media in the first place. Ellsberg ultimately would be criminally prosecuted under the Espionage Act for revealing classified information.

The *Times* went on to publish six more reports on the *Pentagon Papers* and won the ***Pulitzer Prize*** for Public Service in 1972.

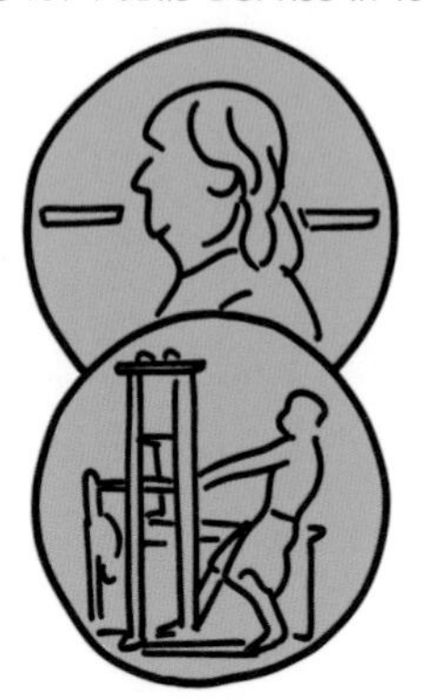

The *Pentagon Papers* revealed that ***four presidents*** had repeatedly and intentionally ***lied*** to the media and the American public about the ***origins, nature,*** and ***extent*** of the Vietnam War.

What had always been a ***fragile*** and ***combative relationship*** between the press and the government had ***fractured*** in a way that would not be healed, leading these two entities down a considerably more ***adversarial path.***

On the war front, the continued publication of the *Pentagon Papers* did not hasten the end of the conflict as much as Ellsberg and other anti-war activists had hoped. America would not withdraw from Vietnam for another ***four years.***

Yet they surely lent credibility to "the growing consensus that the Vietnam War was ***wrong*** and legitimized the radical critique of the war."

END the WAR in VIET NAM

Nixon's unsuccessful fight to stop publication of the *Pentagon Papers* lit a fire under his building ***paranoia*** and desire for ***revenge*** against his perceived enemies.

He authorized the formation of the White House Special Investigations Unit, soon to become infamously known as ***the Plumbers.***

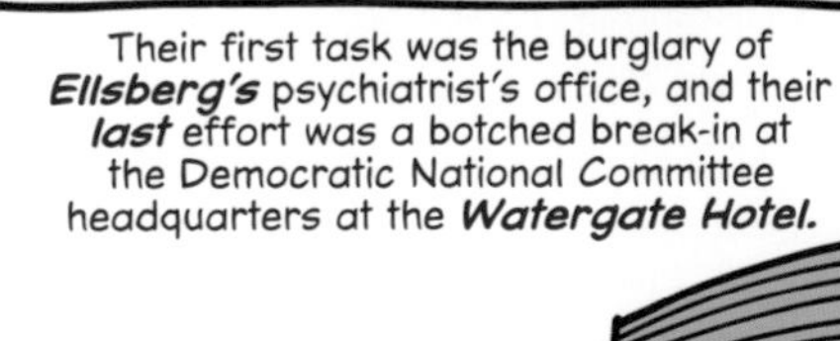

Their first task was the burglary of ***Ellsberg's*** psychiatrist's office, and their ***last*** effort was a botched break-in at the Democratic National Committee headquarters at the ***Watergate Hotel.***

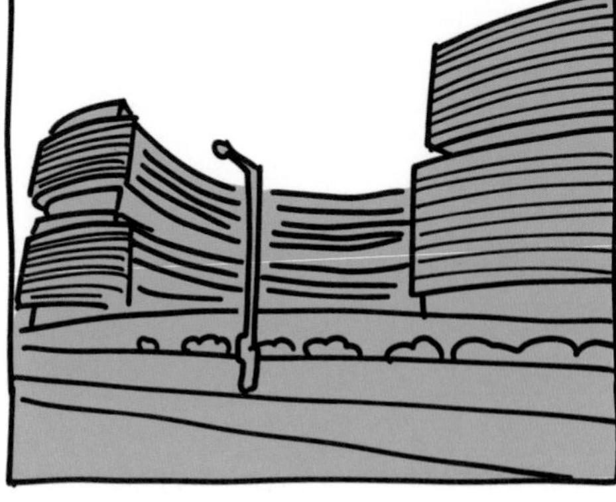

As a result, the judge in Ellsberg's trial would later ***drop*** all charges against him after the evidence of the burglary was put before the court.

Ironically, it was Nixon's efforts to stop the *Pentagon Papers* and leakers at all costs, not anything in the documents or press reports on them, that brought down his presidency and enabled Ellsberg to walk away from any criminal consequences.

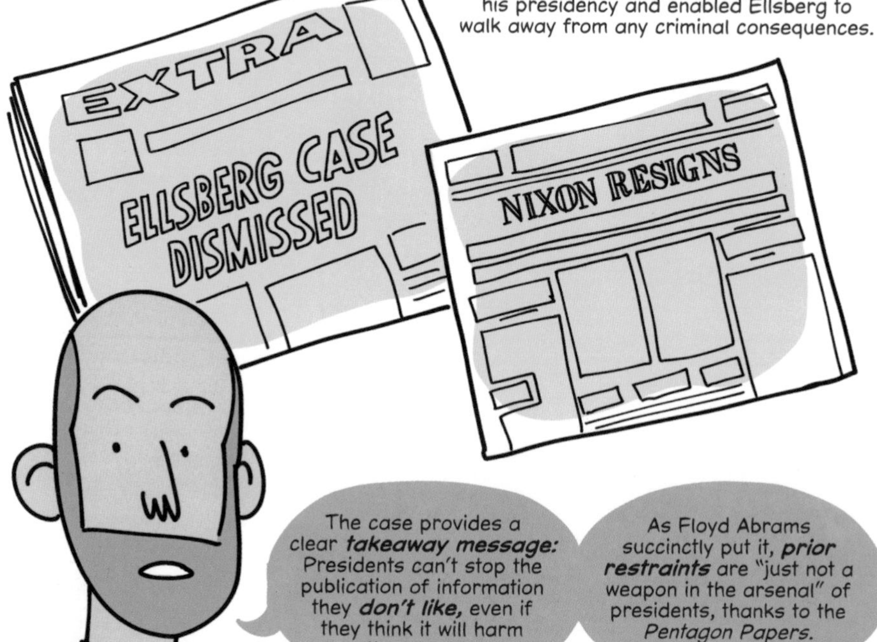
EXTRA
ELLSBERG CASE DISMISSED
NIXON RESIGNS

The case provides a clear ***takeaway message:*** Presidents can't stop the publication of information they ***don't like,*** even if they think it will harm the country.

As Floyd Abrams succinctly put it, ***prior restraints*** are "just not a weapon in the arsenal" of presidents, thanks to the *Pentagon Papers.*

Which brings us back to our contemporary ***conundrum:*** Is President Trump ***constitutionally prohibited*** from obtaining a prior restraint to stop *60 Minutes* from broadcasting an interview with Stormy Daniels?

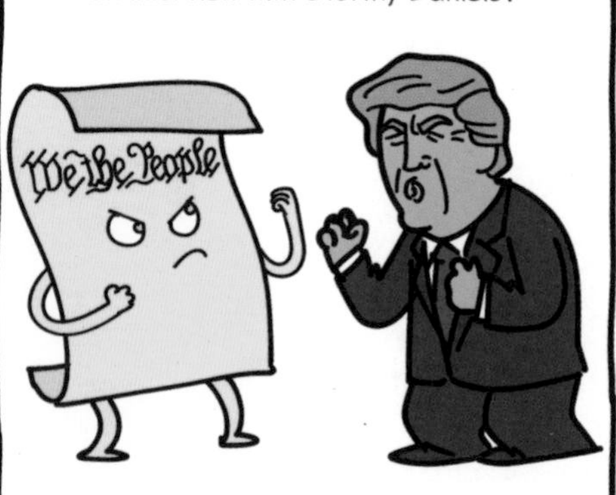
We the People

Trump's legal team began by seeking an ***emergency order*** to enforce her 2016 ***nondisclosure agreement*** and prevent her from disclosing any of the ***confidential information*** it covered.

NDA

They argued that if Daniels wasn't ordered to abide by the agreement, Trump would suffer ***irreparable harm.*** As a result, a temporary restraining order was issued against Daniels, handing Trump a preliminary ***win.***

WINNING

Daniels fought back with a separate legal action to declare the NDA unenforceable because Trump ***never signed*** the agreement. But before these legal fights were concluded, Daniels sat for the interview with Anderson Cooper, the ***broadcast*** of which would enable Daniels to ***break*** her agreement.

Michael Cohen eventually pled guilty to ***criminal campaign finance violations*** for his part in a scheme with Trump to hide Daniels's accusations from voters in the final weeks of the presidential campaign. Prosecutors stressed that Cohen's crimes "struck a blow to one of the core goals of the federal campaign finance laws: ***transparency.***" The federal judge at sentencing agreed that Cohen had done "***insidious harm*** to our democratic institutions" and ordered him to ***three years in prison.***

With Cohen's crimes ***confirmed,*** the question of whether Trump ***broke the law*** working with Cohen to make "hush payoffs" is an undeniably ***relevant*** one.

Nevertheless, Trump's legal team could still argue that a balancing test should be used to weigh privacy and contract rights against those of the press. His lawyers could contend that the potential privacy violation is unusually damaging and the public interest in the material is low.

After all, the argument could continue, why should a media company be allowed to help someone break a ***contractual agreement*** just because the First Amendment might favor publication over restrictions on the press in some cases?

NDA

Thankfully, however, the *Pentagon Papers* precedent, and the string of cases reaffirming its principles over the years, establishes that prior restraints are almost ***always*** unconstitutional.

The PENTAGON PAPERS

It also created a ***legal test*** that does more than just ***balance*** the First Amendment protections against other valid interests. Instead, anyone seeking a prior restraint on the media needs to meet the extremely ***heavy burden*** that broadcast or publication would "surely result in direct, immediate, and irreparable damage to our Nation or its people."

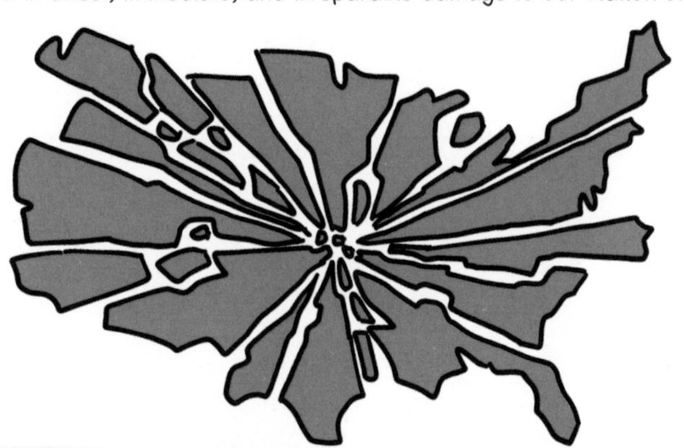

If publishing ***top secret*** government documents during wartime and the resulting potential threats to national security interests were ***not sufficient*** to meet this burden, it is clear that very few factual situations will have any chance of doing so.

In this way, the *Pentagon Papers* continues to be an invaluable, and often unnoticed, ***shield*** for the press against governmental interference in their reporting.

PP

Stormy Daniels and her lawyer likely felt *emboldened* to break her NDA knowing that if she risked talking, he could wield the *Pentagon Papers* against a *conspiracy* to silence her.
PP
Ultimately, *what* Stormy Daniels had to say about Trump's sex life is not as important as her *ability* to say it.

The *Pentagon Papers* case matters because it constrains anyone, all the way up to and including the ***president of the United States,*** from stopping the publication of information they do not like or do not want to be heard.

AIR FORCE

From ***Vietnam secrets*** to claims of ***sexual*** and ***political misconduct,*** the First Amendment continues to mean that the media's ability to speak truth to power is ***unabridged.*** No one can stand in the way of Americans' ability to ***see, hear,*** and then ***judge for ourselves.***

Chapter 6:
FLIPPING OFF THE PRESIDENT AND FUCK THE DRAFT

On a Saturday afternoon in October of 2017, a woman was riding her bike near her home in northern Virginia.

As about a half-dozen vehicles began to slowly drive past her, she realized it was ***President Trump's*** motorcade, leaving the nearby Trump National Golf Course.

"My blood started ***boiling*** at that point," she later recalled. "I lifted my arm and started ***flipping him off.*** I started thinking, you're ***golfing*** again when there is so much going on right now." Afterward, she didn't give it much more thought, never expecting that this fleeting expression of anger was about to change her life.

Unbeknownst to the unidentified woman, members of the ***press corps*** happened to capture the moment of spontaneous protest. A few hours later, the White House bureau chief for ***Voice of America*** tweeted a photograph of the ***"lone cyclist."***

The image quickly became a viral sensation, and was called "the middle-finger salute seen around the world." On *The Late Show*, host ***Stephen Colbert*** quipped, "No one has summed up the ***mood*** of the country better...Long may she wave."

The woman being hailed by Trump's critics as a "she-ro" was ***Juli Briskman,*** a fifty-year-old marketing analyst and a single mother of two teens. The next day, Briskman saw the images on social media and posted them to her ***Twitter*** and ***Facebook*** accounts.

That Monday, Briskman decided to tell her employer that she was the woman in the now famous photo.

One day later, Briskman was ***fired*** and escorted out of the building, taking her personal belongings with her in a box.

It was only ***after*** Briskman lost her job, allegedly for violating the company's ***social media policy,*** that she identified herself to the media. Six months later, she ***sued*** her former employer for ***wrongful termination.***

The challenge facing Briskman's lawsuit is that the First Amendment only protects against ***government*** interference with speech, and ***not*** the actions of private employers. Nevertheless, Briskman's free speech fight highlights captivating questions about whether the First Amendment protects ***nonverbal communication,*** how you communicate a protest message, and the use in public places of ***"unseemly expletives."***

Flashing back to a case from the ***1960s anti-war movement*** will illuminate the extent to which these speech rights are protected—even when ***no words are spoken.***

On April 26, 1968, nineteen-year-old ***Paul Robert Cohen*** entered the Los Angeles County courthouse. Cohen was there to testify in a misdemeanor trial as a defense witness, but ***three police officers*** took particular note of what Cohen was ***wearing.***

FUCK THE DRAFT

Cohen ***removed*** his jacket and folded it over his arm before entering the courtroom.

One of the policemen, ***Sergeant Huston Splawn,*** "sent the presiding judge a note suggesting that Cohen be held in ***contempt of court.***"

The judge ***declined*** to take any action, and so the officer waited until Cohen left the courtroom and then promptly ***arrested him.***

At ***trial,*** Cohen testified that the words on the jacket expressed "the ***depth*** of his feelings against the Vietnam War and the draft." No one claimed that he, or anyone who saw his jacket, had attempted any ***violent action*** in the court building, "nor was there any evidence he uttered any sound prior to his arrest."

Cohen was **convicted** of a California law that prohibited "maliciously and willfully disturb[ing] the peace or quiet of any neighborhood or person...by...offensive conduct" and sentenced to **thirty days in jail.**
His conviction was **affirmed** by the California Court of Appeal, which found that Cohen "carefully chose the **forum** for his views where his conduct would have an effective **shock impact...**[and] was intent upon attracting the attention of others to his views by the **sheer vulgarity** of his expression."

The court **rejected** his First Amendment arguments, asserting that "no one has the right to express his views by means of printing lewd and vulgar language which is likely to cause others to breach the peace to protect **women** and **children** from such exposure."

WORDS

The harsh sentence and the almost palpable disdain toward Cohen can seemingly best be explained by a deeply felt hostility to the language and content of his political message.

FUCK THE DRAFT

This judicial reaction to Cohen's stenciled slogan also reflected how **extremely divided** the country was in 1968, both toward the Vietnam War and the student-led **anti-war movement** that was rising up against it.

Tet Offensive, Jan-Feb 1968.
END the WAR in VIET NAM
I will not **seek,** and I will not **accept** the nomination of my party for another term as your president.
President Lyndon Johnson
It seems now more certain than **ever** that the bloody experience of **Vietnam** is to end in a **stalemate...**
Walter Kronkite

On February 22, 1971, oral argument in ***Cohen v. California*** was about to begin, but ***Chief Justice Warren Burger*** did not want the expletive central to the case to be spoken aloud, and tried to ***communicate*** this to Cohen's attorney, ***Melville Nimmer.***
Chief Justice Warren Burger

Nimmer, a distinguished professor at UCLA School of Law and an expert on copyright, thought he would lose the case if he didn't say ***fuck*** out loud. Using a euphemism would be essentially conceding that the word was indeed ***unspeakable*** in courtrooms and society.

FUDGE!

He decided to take a ***bold stand.*** He would politely ***acknowledge*** the guidance and then just as politely ***ignore it.***

May it please the Court, what this young man did was to walk through a courthouse corridor...wearing a jacket upon which were inscribed the words ***"Fuck the draft."***

As Nimmer said the word in question, "the Chief Justice's face turned a ***bright crimson,*** almost matching the deep red curtains behind the bench."

Nimmer had demonstrated that uttering ***fuck*** before the justices had neither caused ***chaos*** to ensue nor destroyed the ***sanctity*** of the Court. None of the justices, however, would follow his lead and utter the word themselves even ***once*** during questioning.

Nimmer then tried to get the justices more ***comfortable*** with the youth-driven protest movements of the time, which provided the background for Cohen's case. So he cleverly told them they could teach those kids a valuable ***lesson.***

The younger generation tends to "equate ***violent*** dissent and dissent that may be regarded as ***objectionable*** or ***offensive.*** It is terribly important," Nimmer encouraged, "that this Court make clear that ***distinction,*** that dissent by its very nature involves the ***right*** to be offensive.

FUCK THE DRAFT

"But on the other hand ***violent dissent*** is something quite different."

If you punish Cohen for an indisputably ***peaceful protest,*** he was saying, then that leaves nothing to discourage all those hippies from ***turning to violence*** as they continue to express their anti-war messages.

Nimmer also contended that the public deserves to know the "***depth*** of the feeling" that sometimes can most effectively be communicated by ***cursing.***

I DON'T LIKE THE DRAFT

He talked about how "language performs ***two*** functions: there is the ***emotive content*** of the language and there is the ***intellectual content*** of language, and that these intersperse." Forcing Cohen or ***any dissenter*** to express their views without offensive language would rob their speech of its emotive power.

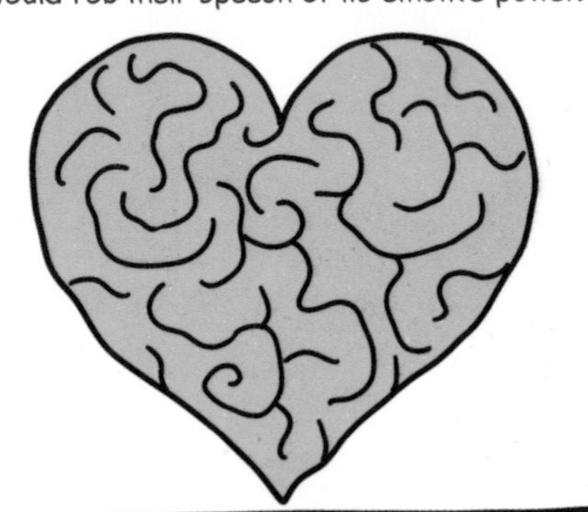

Nimmer asserted that the First Amendment was all about:

"Competition in the ***marketplace of ideas,*** what ideas are going to prevail....

IDEAS!

"But in order for that system to work, it's important that the state ***not*** step in and try to ***censor...*** the ***emotive content...***

IDEAS

"...[because in so doing], the state is thereby enabled...to determine what ideas ***prevail*** in the competition of the market.

"And so for that reason we submit to the Court respectfully that...***offensiveness of form*** no less than ***offensiveness of substance*** must be preserved by the First Amendment if the First Amendment is to be ***meaningful."***

FUCK
THE
DRAFT

Nimmer had ingeniously placed ***fuck*** not at the periphery but at the ***center*** of First Amendment theory, and rarely has the ***marketplace metaphor*** been so persuasively wielded.

FUCK!

Justice Potter Stewart pressed Los Angeles deputy city attorney ***Michael T. Sauer*** to explain, if the California statute prohibited "tumultuous and offensive ***conduct"*** and not ***speech,*** then...

...the ***conduct*** was precisely ***what?***

Displaying the sign on the jacket, by the fact he was walking with the sign displayed on his jacket.

And the ***walking*** wasn't offensive conduct. ***Just the walking*** was it?

Walking ***with the sign.*** Merely walking, ***no.***

And so ***what*** was the ***conduct?***

Displaying the sign.

Displaying?

Yes, his ***conduct*** of ***displaying*** the sign.
The words—
Yes, where other persons were present.

Suppose he had on his jacket..."I dislike the draft."
Then I doubt if we would be here...
So it's a *word* isn't it?...Isn't that all you have?

Well, a *word,* yes.
Sauer seemed not to appreciate that Marshall had gotten him to acknowledge that the state's position boiled down to nothing more than a desire to prohibit the use of a *single word.*

Sauer did manage to end on a strong note. He framed the state's position as, at most, an *inconsequential intrusion* on First Amendment values.
Words of this type are *no essential part* of *any* exposition of ideas, and are of such *slight social value...* that any benefit that may be derived from them is *clearly outweighed* by the social interest in *order* and *morality.*
Nimmer succinctly urged the Court to *reverse* the conviction.
The language of profanity is *not* outside the scope of the First Amendment simply because it's *offensive.*

At the conference following the *Cohen* oral argument, Chief Justice Burger voted to *uphold* Cohen's conviction. Justice Black agreed, telling the group that he viewed Cohen's action as *conduct* and not *speech.* Justices Blackmun and White voted with them as well.

Justice Stewart and the liberal members of the Court—Justices Douglas, Brennan, and Marshall—all voted to *reverse.*

The justices were evenly divided and the deciding vote belonged to the "ideologically independent" Justice Harlan.

By the next conference, Harlan had made up his mind to ***reverse the conviction.*** The vote would be 5 to 4, and Harlan was assigned to write the decision.

Harlan began by sweeping away "what the case is ***not*** about." He swiftly ***dismisses*** the idea that California was regulating ***conduct,*** writing, "The only 'conduct' which the State sought to punish is ***the fact of communication.*** Thus, we deal here with a conviction resting solely upon ***speech.***"

FUCK THE DRAFT

He goes on to remind everyone that "the State certainly lacks power to punish Cohen for the underlying ***content*** of the message the inscription conveyed...[about] the inutility or immorality of the draft..."

He explains that the use of the word ***fuck*** did not fall into any category in which the First Amendment permitted limits on speech. The word is not ***"obscenity"*** (because it is not erotic), or ***"fighting words"*** (because it was not directed at any person), nor a ***"captive"*** audience problem (because it took place in public, rather than causing an "intrusion into the privacy of the home").

OBSCENITY
VIOLENCE
PRIVACY

Harlan presents the case as ***really*** being about the state's efforts to "remove this offensive word from the public vocabulary."

He rejected the idea that the use of the word "is inherently likely to cause ***violent reaction.***" Referring to the ***Tinker*** case, he states that "undifferentiated fear or apprehension of disturbance...is ***not*** enough to overcome the right to freedom of expression."

He also raised the ***broader notion*** of whether the government should have a role in "acting as guardians of ***public morality.***"

The constitutional right of free expression is powerful medicine in a society as diverse and populous as ours.
It is designed and intended to remove governmental restraints from the arena of public discussion, putting the decision as to what views shall be voiced largely into the hands of each of us...

...in the hope that use of such freedom will ultimately produce a more capable citizenry and more perfect polity and in the belief that no other approach would comport with the premise of individual dignity and choice upon which our political system rests.
To many, the immediate consequence of this freedom may often appear to be only verbal tumult, discord, and even offensive utterance.
GO!
COMPLY
RESIST
STOP!
YES!
NO!

DEBATE

These are, however, within **established limits,** in truth **necessary side effects** of the broader enduring values which the process of open debate permits us to achieve.
That the air may at times seem filled with **verbal cacophony** is, in this sense not a sign of weakness but of **strength.**
We cannot lose sight of the fact that, in what otherwise might seem a **trifling** and **annoying** instance of individual **distasteful abuse** of a privilege, these fundamental **societal values** are truly implicated.

How is one to distinguish this from any other offensive word?...Surely the State has **no right** to cleanse public debate to the point where it is grammatically palatable to the most **squeamish** among us.

SOAP

And then, in one of the **most famous** First Amendment lines of all time, Harlan recognizes that although **fuck** may be worse than most curse words...

...it is nevertheless often true that one man's **vulgarity** is another's **lyric.**

Fuck

Words are often chosen as much for their **emotive** as their **cognitive** force, [and] that emotive function...may often be the more **important** element of the overall message sought to be communicated.

As a result, Harlan insisted, the emotive power of cursing must not be criminalized.

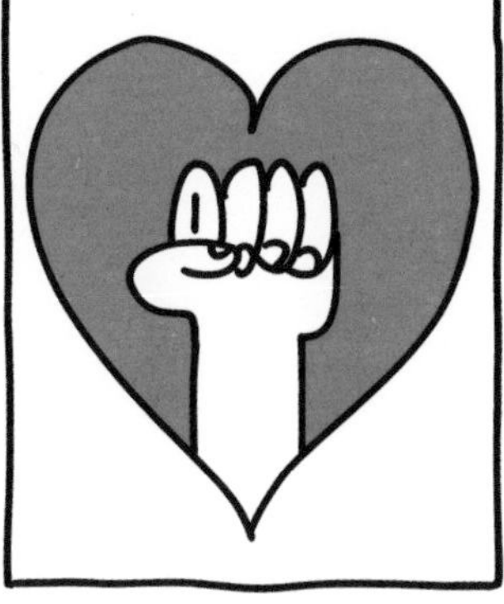

It would be a "facile assumption," Harlan points out, "that one can forbid ***particular words*** without also running a substantial risk of suppressing ***ideas*** in the process."

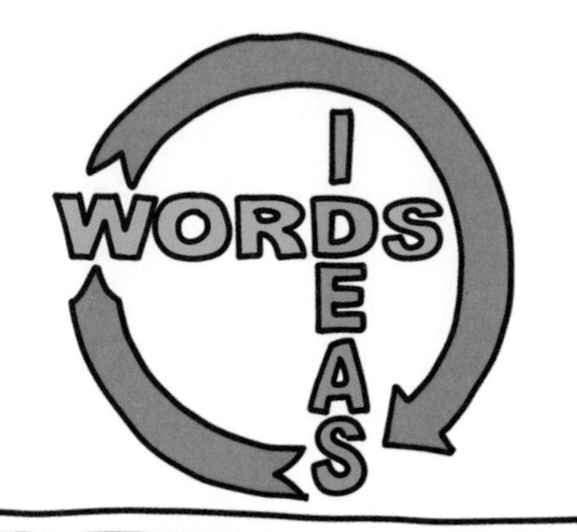
WORDS
IDEAS

That risk would become even greater if there were no check on government power that "might soon seize upon the censorship of particular words as a convenient ***guise*** for banning the expression of ***unpopular views.***"

NO!

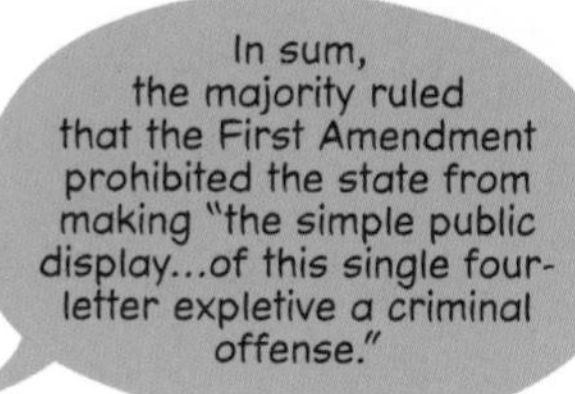
In sum, the majority ruled that the First Amendment prohibited the state from making "the simple public display...of this single four-letter expletive a criminal offense."

The dissent, written by Justice Blackmun and joined by Chief Justice Black, and partially by Justice White, was limited in scope and reasoning. Only two paragraphs long, it lashed out at "Cohen's ***absurd*** and ***immature*** antic," rejecting it without explanation as "mainly ***conduct,*** and little ***speech.***"

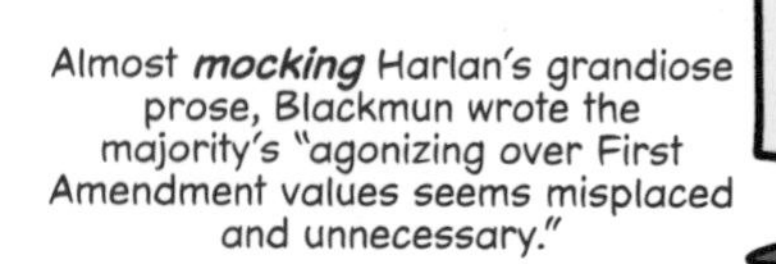
Almost ***mocking*** Harlan's grandiose prose, Blackmun wrote the majority's "agonizing over First Amendment values seems misplaced and unnecessary."

The ***sparseness*** of the dissent may have contributed to the enduring ***strength*** of the majority opinion in ***Cohen*** over the years. The decision stands for ***two*** crucial free speech principles.

Offensive speech, including but not limited to curse words, is as fully entitled to First Amendment protection as ***any other*** speech.

Just as importantly, in public places it is the ***speaker's*** right to ***choose the language*** they feel is ***most effective to communicate*** their message. These concepts go hand in hand to create significant free speech rights for protesters, even when they are not speaking at all.

Juli Briskman's wrongful termination lawsuit was eventually dismissed. ***Cohen v. California*** makes unconstitutional any governmental punishment for giving the finger, but the First Amendment offers ***no protection*** to private sector employees who express their free speech rights, even during personal time and outside of the workplace.

Briskman lost her job but received many offers of employment and was soon working again. What would be ***next*** for this social media symbol of rude resistance to Trump?

Public office. Briskman ran for a seat on her local County Board of Supervisors in Loudoun, Virginia. Her opponent was an incumbent Republican who campaigned for Trump.

I've gotten some feedback that folks say you should ***respect*** the president. Even if you don't like what they're ***doing,*** you shouldn't show this sort of ***disdain.***

And I simply ***disagree,*** and I think the Constitution grants me that privilege.

Many voters must have felt ***similarly,*** since Briskman ***won*** her race and was elected with more than 52% of the vote.

Chapter 7: SAMANTHA BEE, SEVEN DIRTY WORDS, AND INDECENCY

Samantha Bee, the host and executive producer of TBS's late-night news show *Full Frontal with Samantha Bee* has a unique gift for expressing ***outrage.*** She focuses her indignant ire on the weekly political scene with ***ferocious wit*** and a ***feminist perspective.*** A recurring feature on *Full Frontal* are Bee's furious, extended takedowns of mostly conservative politicians.

On ***May 30, 2018,*** when she set her sights on the Trump administration's ***immigration and family separation policies***—criticizing the president, Chief of Staff John Kelly, and Secretary of Homeland Security Kirstjen Nielsen—it seemed like business as usual.

Bee began to wrap up the segment, saying that "most Americans are finally paying attention" to this issue, with one notable ***exception.*** She called out ***Ivanka Trump*** for posting an "oblivious" photo with her ***son*** on Twitter that week.

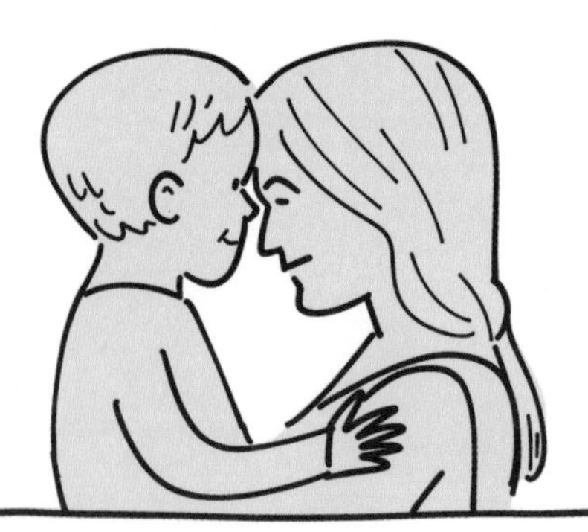

You know, Ivanka, that's a beautiful photo of you and your child. Let me just say, one mother to another, do something about your dad's immigration practices, you feckless cunt. He listens to you.

The ***outrage*** over this use of the ***c-word*** was swift and severe.

[Bee's] disgusting comments and show are ***not fit*** for broadcast, and executives at Time Warner and TBS must demonstrate that such ***explicit profanity*** about female members of this administration will not be condoned on its network.

TE HOUSE
GTON
White House press secretary Sarah Huckabee Sanders

Bee did apologize later that day to Ivanka Trump and viewers, but a day later ***President Trump*** tweeted:

Why aren't they ***firing*** no talent Samantha Bee for the horrible language used on her low ratings show?

Bee would make a ***further apology*** in her next episode, saying that she "should've known that a ***pottymouthed insult*** would be inherently more interesting... than a ***juvenile immigration policy.***"

Meanwhile, one threshold issue that ***went unmentioned*** in this furious news cycle was: Are there words that you really ***can't say*** on television?

Fittingly, the answer to this question comes directly from ***another*** comedian whose words ***shocked*** and ***delighted*** audiences in equal measure.

In 1972, the countercultural comedian ***George Carlin*** recorded his third album, *Class Clown.* The last track on the record was called ***"Seven Words You Can Never Say on Television."***

GEORGE CARLIN
CLASS CLOWN

There are four hundred thousand words in the English language and there are seven of them you can't say on television. What a ratio that is! Three hundred ninety-nine thousand nine hundred and ninety-three...to seven!
They must really be bad. They'd have to be outrageous to be separated from a group that large.
"All of you over here...You seven, you bad words." That's what they told us, you remember? "That's a bad word." What?
There are no bad words. Bad thoughts, bad intentions, but no bad words.
You know the seven, don't you, that you can't say on television? Shit, piss, fuck, cunt, cocksucker, motherfucker, and tits.
Those are the Heavy Seven. Those are the ones that'll infect your soul, curve your spine, and keep the country from winning the war.

The material epitomized Carlin's new approach of challenging societal norms by engaging in hilariously transgressive wordplay, and it would help to make him a comic legend.
Carlin later observed that Lenny Bruce "was the first one to make language an issue, and he suffered for it. I was the first one to make language an issue and succeed with it."
Lenny Bruce
Carlin performed the routine in his hometown at Carnegie Hall and received a standing ovation.
However, it would not play so well with every audience, and he soon found that "not only could you not say the Heavy Seven on television, you couldn't say them in Milwaukee, either."
On July 21, 1972, Carlin launched into his "Seven Words" before a Summerfest crowd of 35,000. An indignant Milwaukee police officer couldn't believe his ears and Carlin was arrested as he left the stage. The photo became front-page news and was carried all over the country.

Eventually, the charge of disorderly conduct was dismissed after a trial in which the judge reportedly ***"laughed softly,*** though self-consciously," while listening to the cut from a record player set up in the courtroom.

Emboldened by his victory and building on the words that he gleefully referred to as the ***Milwaukee Seven,*** Carlin soon developed an "equally mind-rotting, spinecurving, peace-without-honor sequel called ***'Filthy Words.'"***
FILTHY WORDS

I was thinking one night about the words you couldn't say on the public, ah, airwaves, um, the ones you ***definitely*** wouldn't say, ever...and it came down to seven but the list is open to ***amendment...***
...a lot of people pointed things out to me, and I noticed some ***myself.*** The original seven words were shit, piss, fuck, cunt, cocksucker, motherfucker, and tits.
GEORGE CARLIN OCCUPATION: FOOLE
And now the first thing that we noticed was that word ***fuck*** was really ***repeated*** in there because the word ***motherfucker*** is a ***compound word*** and it's another form of the word ***fuck.***
You want to be a ***purist,*** it doesn't really, it can't be on the list of basic words.
And it continued on in this way for about another ***eleven minutes.***

On **October 30, 1973,** at two o'clock in the afternoon, "Filthy Words" was played on radio station **WBAI** in New York, part of the listener-supported Pacifica Network.

WBAI

The recording was included during an episode of a live program called **Lunch Pail,** about "the power of language and how words lose integrity during political debate."
Before Carlin's track was played, the host, Paul Gorman, warned "that it included sensitive language which might be regarded as offensive to some; those who might be offended were advised to change the station and return to WBAI in fifteen minutes."

A man named **John Douglas** said he heard the broadcast while driving with his **"young son."** Douglas ended up sending a **complaint** to the **Federal Communications Commission** (FCC) stating that "any child could have been turning the dial, and tuned in to that garbage." Not a **single other complaint** was received by the station or the FCC.

It turns out that Douglas was not exactly a typical **disinterested listener,** as he is often portrayed, but rather an **advocate** who was on the national planning board of an organization called **Morality in Media.** He also later admitted that he didn't just happen upon the program, but rather "was listening to Pacifica **constantly** to see how far they would pull the curtain back."

MIM

MORALITY IN MEDIA, inc

In addition, his ***"young son"*** was, in fact, fifteen years old, and they were returning home from a college tour of ***Yale.*** Carlin called Douglas "a professional ***offendee."***

Douglas's ***partisan*** nature notwithstanding, his lone complaint successfully triggered a ***seismic change*** in the regulation of radio and television content.

The ***FCC*** is a federal agency that was created by Congress in the ***Communications Act of 1934*** to regulate broadcasting in the ***public interest.*** Both the Communications Act and the First Amendment "***prohibits*** the Commission from ***censoring*** broadcast material and from ***interfering*** with ***freedom of expression*** in broadcasting."

FEDERAL COMMUNICATIONS
COMMISSION
US

However, the agency can place ***restrictions*** on the material that stations broadcast. The enforcement of these restrictions on objectionable content is driven by ***complaints*** from the public.

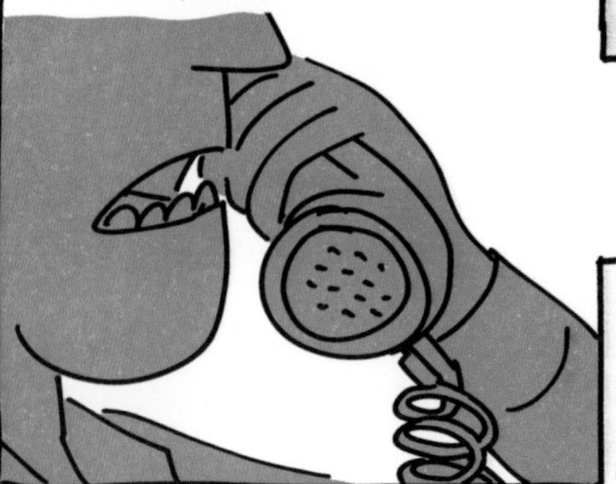

The ***FCC Enforcement Bureau*** reviews complaints and then decides whether to launch an ***investigation*** if its staff believes a violation may have occurred.

ENFORCEMENT BUREAU

If the FCC ultimately finds a violation of its ***indecency rules,*** it may issue a ***warning,*** impose a ***fine,*** or even ***revoke*** a station's license to operate.

The FCC forwarded Douglas's complaint to the station with a request for comments. Pacifica strongly ***defended*** including the recording in their broadcast, which they described as "devoted to an analysis of the use of language in contemporary society."

COMPLAINT

WBAI

Pacifica also championed Carlin as "a significant ***social satirist*** of American manners and language in the tradition of Mark Twain" and sought to ***contextualize*** his choice of words.

Carlin is not mouthing obscenities, he is merely using words to satirize as harmless and essentially silly our attitudes towards those words. As with other great satirists...Carlin often grabs our attention by speaking the unspeakable, by shocking in order to illuminate.

More than a ***year later,*** and without articulating a ***clear rule,*** the FCC declared that Carlin's language in the broadcast was ***indecent*** given that it "describes, in terms patently offensive as measured by contemporary community standards for the broadcast medium, sexual or excretory activities and organs, at times of the day when there is a reasonable risk that ***children*** may be in the audience."

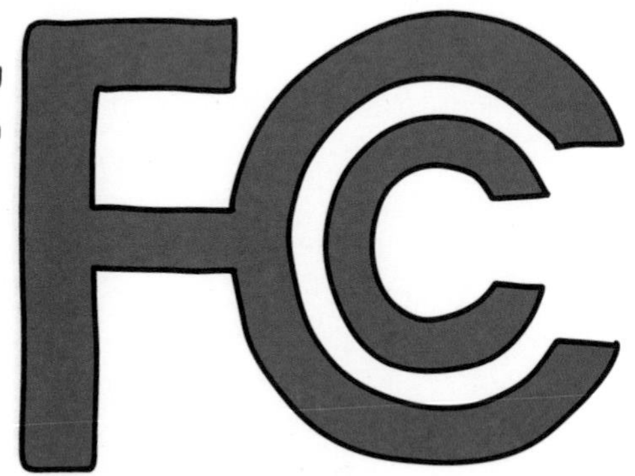
FCC

The FCC brushed aside any consideration of ***artistic merit*** or ***political message,*** staking a claim that it had the ***authority*** to regulate such language. The agency implicitly acknowledged that this was breaking ***new ground,*** by imposing ***no penalty*** and stating the order was intended to clarify the ***standards*** to be considered in the "growing number" of indecent speech complaints.

Pacifica appealed to the **United States Court of Appeals for the District of Columbia Circuit.** The Circuit **reversed** the FCC's order, by a 2-to-1 majority, holding that the FCC's order was "**censorship,** regardless of what the Commission chooses to call it," and its direct effect was "to **inhibit** the free and robust exchange of **ideas.**"
UNITED STATES COURT OF APPEALS
DISTRICT OF COLUMBIA CIRCUIT
As for the FCC's professed goal of protecting the sensitivities of **children,** the court found that such a kid-centered approach would go too far in limiting what **adults** could hear and was "a classic case of burning the **house** to roast the **pig.**"
The Circuit also refused the FCC's additional claim that the uniquely **intrusive nature** of radio and television **justified** regulations, noting that "the impact of a particular medium constitutes **no basis** for subjecting that medium to **greater suppression.**"
This time it was the FCC that decided to **appeal,** despite the fact that some there thought **losing** before the Supreme Court was **likely.** The primary question before the justices in ***FCC v. Pacifica Foundation*** was whether the First Amendment prohibited the FCC from restricting the broadcast of indecent language that was **not obscene.**

Obscenity, the Supreme Court had ruled five years earlier, was content so offensive that it was not protected by the First Amendment at all, if "the work, taken as a whole, appeals to the prurient interest" (meaning inappropriate sexual desire), "depicts or describes, in a patently offensive way, sexual conduct," and "lacks serious literary, artistic, political, or scientific value."
At oral argument before the Supreme Court, the most telling moment came right as Chief Justice Warren began, "You may bear in mind that we are familiar with the facts of the case and get directly at your legal argument if you wish."
This suggestion was a not-so-subtle warning: "Don't repeat any dirty words in this court!" It was not a good sign for the broadcasters.

On July 3, 1978, a divided Court ruled in favor of the FCC, holding in a 5-to-4 decision that the agency had the power to regulate even isolated words in otherwise protected speech.

Writing for the narrow majority, Justice John Paul Stevens found that the "broadcast of patently offensive words dealing with sex and excretion" had "such slight social value...that any benefit that may be derived from them is clearly outweighed by the social interest in order and morality."

Having ***minimized*** the importance of the speech based on the ***words used,*** rather than the ***content*** of the ***entire work,*** Stevens set forth ***two*** main rationales for allowing speech restrictions in these circumstances. First, he determined that the ***unique nature*** of the broadcast medium enabled the government to treat such speech ***differently*** in order to ***shield*** citizens from its impact.

For Stevens, broadcast media's "***pervasive presence*** in the lives of all Americans" meant that "indecent material presented over the airwaves confronts the citizen not only in ***public,*** but also in the ***privacy*** of the ***home.***"
OFF

In addition, since broadcast audiences were "constantly tuning ***in*** and tuning ***out,***" Stevens believed that warnings were so ***ineffective*** that to say, "one may avoid further offense by turning off the radio when he hears indecent language is like saying that the remedy for an assault is to run away ***after*** the ***first blow.***"

Secondly, Stevens bemoaned that broadcasting was "uniquely accessible to ***children,*** even those too young to read," and that protecting America's youth from indecent content necessitated "restricting the expression ***at its source.***"
STATION

In *dissent,* Justice Brennan, joined by Justice Marshall, described themselves as "unable to remain silent" in the face of the majority's flagrant *"misapplication* of fundamental First Amendment principles." Brennan dismissed Stevens's concerns about intrusions in the home as *trivial:*
Justice Marshall
Whatever the *minimal discomfort* suffered by a listener who inadvertently tunes in to a program he finds offensive during the brief interval before he can simply *extend his arm* and switch stations or flick the *"off"* button, it is surely worth the candle to preserve the broadcaster's right to *send,* and the right of those interested to *receive,* a message *entitled* to full First Amendment *protection.*
Justice Brennan
Brennan found the "children in the audience" rationale equally *unpersuasive,* insisting that such sweeping treatment impermissibly results in "reduc[ing] the adult population...to [hearing] only what is fit for children."
FUCK THE DRAFT
Brennan also took issue with Stevens's seemingly cavalier attitude toward the Court's decision in *Cohen v. California* just seven years earlier. Brennan pointed out that the privacy interests of *listeners* to the radio are "surely *no greater* than those of the *people present* in the corridor of the Los Angeles courthouse in *Cohen* who bore witness to the *words...* emblazoned across *Cohen's jacket."*

More crucially, Brennan rebuked Stevens for ignoring the ***central message of Cohen,*** that "even if an alternative phrasing may communicate a speaker's ***abstract ideas*** as ***effectively*** as those words he is forbidden to use, it is doubtful that the sterilized message will convey the ***emotion*** that is an essential part of so many communications."

Brennan called out the majority for engaging in "another of the ***dominant culture's*** inevitable efforts to force those groups who do not share its mores to ***conform*** to its way of thinking, acting, and speaking."

Despite Brennan's passionate ***dissent,*** and the fact that regulating the content of speech seems at odds with the ***spirit*** of the First Amendment, ***Pacifica*** remains the ***law*** of radio and television broadcasts to this day. The FCC has the ***power to restrict*** when language or images of "sexual or excretory organs or activities" that it finds "patently offensive" can air, and to ***fine*** stations for that material.

FCC

18+
ADULT
CONTENT

The FCC ***prohibits*** indecent speech between the hours of ***6 AM to 10 PM,*** during which time it considers that there is a ***"reasonable*** risk that children may be in the audience." The FCC leaves the remaining time period as a ***"safe harbor"*** for unregulated (meaning more ***"adult"***) content.

After winning the right to control and punish content it found offensive, the FCC then made ***no effort*** to exercise its newly recognized powers for nearly a ***decade.*** The FCC's post-***Pacifica*** restraint lasted until the late 1980s when ***Howard Stern*** became a new favorite target.

The Howard Stern Show

The agency then issued a series of ***indecency violations*** against ***Infinity Broadcasting,*** which syndicated Howard Stern's radio show, for incidents including: Stern taunting the agency by saying, "Hey, FCC, ***'penis,'"*** joking about ***masturbating*** to a picture of Aunt Jemima, or discussing another man playing the piano with his penis.

Infinity Broadcasting ultimately ended up calling it ***quits*** on its seven-year legal war with the FCC, and paid a then-record ***$1.71 million fine*** to settle the matters, but with no admission of wrongdoing.

The next major wave of FCC actions was triggered by a series of celebrities ***cursing*** spontaneously on awards shows.

I've also had my critics for the last forty years saying that I was on my way out every year. Right. So fuck 'em.
Cher
2002 Billboard Music Awards
Have you ever tried to get cow shit out of a Prada purse? It's not so fucking simple.
Nicole Richie
2003 Billboard Music Awards
This is really, really fucking brilliant.
Bono
2003 Golden Globes

The FCC found all of these ***indecent,*** holding that the ***f-word*** was "one of the most ***vulgar, graphic*** and ***explicit descriptions*** of sexual activity in the English language," and therefore "any use of that word or a variation, in ***any context,*** inherently has a sexual connotation."

At the same time, the FCC became determinedly concerned with ***"fleeting nudity"*** as well. A 2003 broadcast of the police drama *NYPD Blue* showing "the nude buttocks of an adult female character for approximately seven seconds and for a moment the side of her breast" was also found indecent.

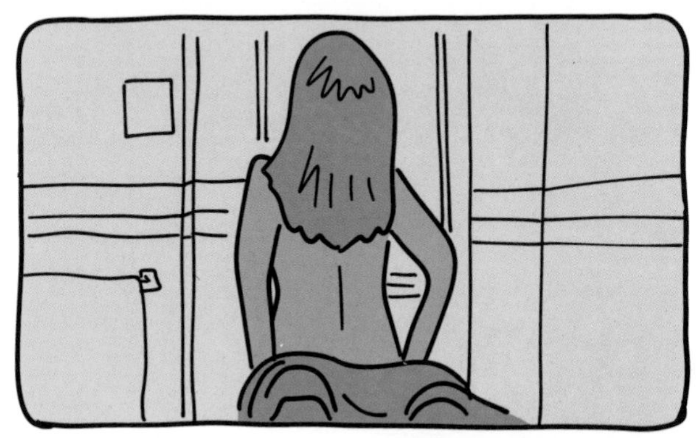

The FCC was even more scandalized by the infamous ***"wardrobe malfunction"*** during the ***2004 Super Bowl halftime show,*** in which ***Justin Timberlake*** sang, "Bet I'll have you naked by the end of this song," and then exposed ***Janet Jackson's*** breast for 9/16 of a second.

After receiving more than 500,000 complaints, the FCC fined CBS the then-maximum penalty of $27,500 per violation against each of the twenty television stations owned by CBS, for a total of $550,000.

Even that was not enough for Congress, which later passed the Broadcast Decency Enforcement Act largely in reaction to the Super Bowl debacle. The law raised the top fine to a whopping $325,000 per violation or a maximum of $3 million for the same violation that aired on multiple stations.

The convoluted process of FCC actions and network appeals concerning these incidents would not reach the Supreme Court for a final resolution until ***2012.***

In the fleeting expletives and *NYPD Blue* case, known as ***FCC v. Fox,*** a unanimous Court ruled in favor of the ***networks*** and set aside the FCC's orders. The Court held that the agency had failed to provide ***"fair notice"*** to broadcasters over the change in policy that ***"fleeting expletives*** and ***momentary nudity*** could be found actionably indecent."

FCC
V.
FOX

In the ***FCC v. CBS*** case concerning the Super Bowl scandal, the Supreme Court ***upheld*** the Third Circuit Court's ruling, which found, ***again,*** that the FCC had failed to give ***reasonable notice*** of the change in policy. The ruling served to ***invalidate*** the FCC's fine against CBS.

FCC
V.
CBS

However, in an unusual ***separate opinion,*** Chief Justice John Roberts wrote to emphasize that going forward ***all necessary notice*** had been ***delivered.***

Words or ***images,*** no matter how brief or arguably nonsexual, can be regulated by the FCC such that broadcasters could face millions of dollars in indecency fines for a single slip of the tongue or clothing.

Why isn't ***Pacifica*** a major problem then for ***Samantha Bee?*** The ***c-word*** must still be ***indecent*** by FCC standards, and such ***fleeting uses*** are no longer an exception to FCC indecency regulation.

The program airs at 9:30 PM in the central time zone, so it does not fall into the late-night ***safe harbor.*** How could the show escape FCC censure and ***huge fines?***

18+
ADULT
CONTENT

The answer is ***simple*** and makes little ***practical sense.*** The FCC does not regulate indecency on ***cable*** at all—neither ***basic cable*** nor ***premium channels.*** The FCC has explained its lack of authority to regulate indecency on cable and satellite television based on the fact that they are ***"subscription services"*** and the statutory language regarding "radio communications" applies only to ***broadcast channels.***

BROADCAST
PUBLIC
AIRWAVES

PRIVATE
SYSTEMS
SUBSCRIPTION

Arguably, these are distinctions ***without*** a difference, particularly in our current ***platform-agnostic age*** of content ***everywhere.*** Nevertheless, the FCC's indecency regime still ***does not extend*** to cable and satellite TV.

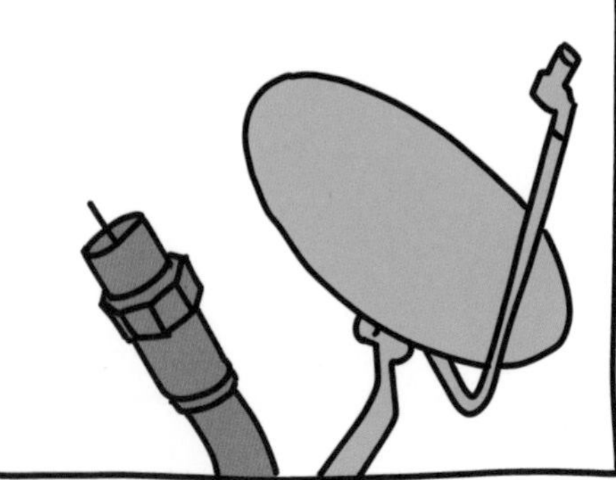

The result is that Samantha Bee is ***free*** to say a word that would almost ***certainly*** subject her broadcast colleagues to ***massive*** indecency fines.

The comment ended up as little more than a ***temporary setback*** for Bee and her team. A month later, *Full Frontal* was nominated for ***seven Emmy awards.***

As for ***Carlin,*** he reflected that he took ***"perverse pride,"*** in the fact that ***FCC v. Pacifica Foundation*** has become a ***standard case*** to teach in communications classes and many ***law schools.***

I'm actually a footnote to the judicial history of America.

Carlin's ***"Seven Dirty Words"*** continue to resonate beyond the classroom to this day, not only because he dared to ***swear,*** but for the way he jubilantly drew attention to the ***absurdity*** of our ***language taboos*** in the face of an American society racked by ***cultural upheaval*** and ***war.***

Bee certainly shares Carlin's concerns about the ***hypocrisy of politeness*** in the face of devastating ***political realities.***

Look, if you are worried about the death of civility, don't sweat it...Civility is just nice words. Maybe we should all worry a little bit more about the niceness of our actions.

In cultural historian ***Melissa Mohr's*** enlightening book, she advocates seriously for accepting the use of ***all kinds*** of words:

HOLY SH*T
A BRIEF HISTORY OF SWEARING
MELISSA MOHR
A healthy society needs its "good" language and its "bad." We need irreproachably formal and unassailably decent speech, but we also need the dirty, the vulgar, the wonderful obscenities and oaths that can do for us what no other words can.

Carlin and Bee, one can assume, would ***approve.***

Chapter 8:

SATURDAY NIGHT LIVE, HUSTLER, AND THE POWER OF PARODY

Donald Trump has been obsessed with *Saturday Night Live* for years. He is the only politician to have hosted the show ***twice***—first as a ***reality television star*** in 2004, and then as a ***presidential candidate*** in 2015.

He ***tweeted*** about the ratings for his second hosting gig five separate times, and bragged that his appearance had garnered *SNL* its ***"best ratings in 4 years!"***

Yet Trump's love affair with *SNL* was ***short-lived.*** Just a few weeks before the election, Trump tweeted:

Watched Saturday Night Live hit job on me. Time to retire the boring and unfunny show. Alec Baldwin portrayal stinks. Media rigging election!

A month later, despite his ***election victory,*** Trump was venting:

I watched parts of @nbcsnl Saturday Night Live last night. It is a totally one-sided, biased show—nothing funny at all. Equal time for us?

Totally biased, not funny and the Baldwin impersonation just can't get any worse.

@NBCNews is bad but Saturday Night Live is the worst of NBC...always a complete hit job.

It is just a political ad for the Dems.

President Trump's escalating **fury** toward *SNL* was evident in his increasingly **explicit calls** to bring federal power to bear on the television program. He wanted **legal action** taken.
A REAL scandal is the one-sided coverage, hour by hour, of networks like NBC & Democrat spin machines like Saturday Night Live. It is all nothing less than unfair news coverage and Dem commercials. Should be tested in courts, can't be legal? Only defame & belittle! Collusion?

Trump next raised the specter of ***reprisals*** against NBC.

How do the Networks get away with these total Republican hit jobs without retribution?

He then even went so far as to threaten a government investigation of the entertainment series.

It's truly incredible that shows like Saturday Night Live, not funny/no talent, can spend all of their time knocking the same person (me), over & over, without so much of a mention of "the other side." Like an advertisement without consequences. Same with Late Night Shows.... Should Federal Election Commission and/or FCC look into this? There must be Collusion with the Democrats and, of course, Russia!

Although it's ***debatable*** whether *SNL*'s mockery of President Trump is any ***harsher*** than their treatment of past presidents (for example, some have argued that ***Chevy Chase's*** portrayal of ***President Gerald Ford*** as a bumbling fool contributed to his losing the election), his public attacks on the program are ***unprecedented*** for a president.

Representative ***Ted Lieu*** rebuked the president on Twitter: "One thing that ***makes America great*** is that the people can laugh at you without ***retribution.*** The First Amendment allows Saturday Night Live to make fun of you again, and again, and ***again.***"

Can satire ***ever*** be so offensive that the injured party would be able to successfully sue for hurt ***feelings?*** Unfortunately for Trump the ***television critic,*** the Supreme Court has seen far more ***vicious humor*** before, in the case of the "***preacher*** versus the ***pornographer.***"

The year was 1983. ***Campari,*** the Italian aperitif, was running a ***risqué*** advertising campaign featuring actors—such as Elizabeth Ashley, Jill St. John, and Tony Roberts—talking about their "***first time.***" ***Double entendres*** abounded, and it all sounded like they were dishing about ***sex.***

Jill St. John talks about her first time.
CAMPARI
You'll never forget your first time.

Jerry Falwell talks about his first time.*
CAMPARI
You'll never forget your first time.
*

On the inside front cover of the November 1983 issue of *Hustler* magazine, published by ***Larry Flynt,*** there was a similar-looking Campari ad featuring a dignified photograph of the famous televangelist ***Jerry Falwell.*** In a fake interview, Reverend Falwell is portrayed as saying that his "first time" was a ***drunken tryst*** with his ***mother*** in an ***outhouse.*** Shockingly, the more you read, the ***worse*** it gets.

FALWELL: I never really expected to make it with Mom, but then after she showed all the other guys in town such a good time, I figured, "What the hell!"

INTERVIEWER: But your mom? Isn't that a bit odd?

FALWELL: I don't think so. Looks don't mean that much to me in a woman.

INTERVIEWER: Go on.

FALWELL: Well, we were drunk off our God-fearing asses on Campari, ginger ale and soda—that's called a Fire and Brimstone—at the time. And Mom looked better than a Baptist whore with a $100 donation.

INTERVIEWER: Campari in the crapper with Mom... how interesting. Well, how was it?

FALWELL: The Campari was great, but Mom passed out...

Falwell's last line returns to the subject of trying Campari again:

FALWELL: Oh, yeah. I always get sloshed before I go out to the pulpit. You don't think I could lay down all that bullshit sober, do you?

At the very bottom, underneath the Campari logo, in small print, a final line reads:

AD PARODY–NOT TO BE TAKEN SERIOUSLY.

In addition, in *Hustler's* table of contents for the issue, the page is similarly described as:

Fiction: Ad and Personality Parody.

It is safe to say that ***neither*** disclaimer provided much ***comfort*** for Jerry Falwell.

In response, Falwell sent out ***three mailings,*** some of which contained a copy of the ad parody, to more than a million of his supporters, attacking "the billion-dollar sex industry, of which Larry Flynt is a self-declared leader...For those porno peddlers, it appears that lust and greed have replaced decency and morality."

Falwell concluded his letters by asking:

"Will you help me defend my family and myself against the smears and slander of this major pornographic magazine—will you send a gift of $500 so that we may take up this important legal battle?"

In a month, Falwell raised more than ***$1 million*** for his litigation war chest. He soon sued Flynt, saying it was because the ad "besmirched the memory of my dear mother."

$1,000,000

Relishing the fight, Flynt published the ad parody ***again*** in *Hustler's* March 1984 issue, while the case moved forward to trial.

To fully comprehend the almost ***apocalyptic*** nature of this ***free speech war,*** it is necessary to examine the personal histories of the two men leading their ***diametrically opposed*** organizations.

In 1956, when Jerry Falwell was twenty-two years old, he founded the ***Thomas Road Baptist Church*** in Lynchburg, Virginia. What began with a congregation of thirty-five people would expand to 1,000 members a year later, and to more than 20,000 in the 1980s and beyond.

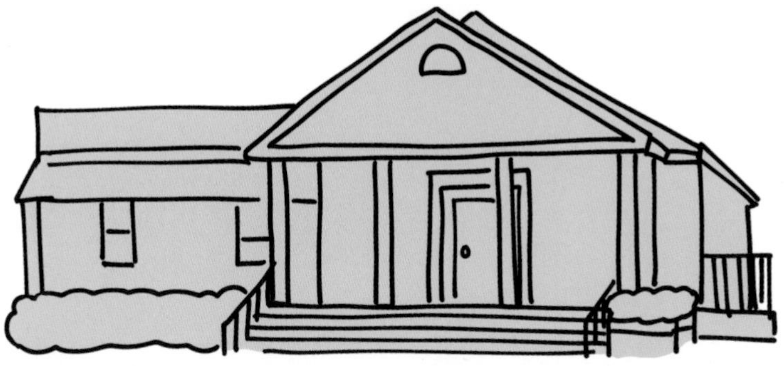

The church also grew to include ***a school, summer camp, home for alcoholics, international missions,*** and ***Liberty University,*** an "accredited evangelical liberal arts institution."

Six months after founding his church, he began broadcasting the *Old-Time Gospel Hour* on radio and television, developing a nationwide following that would eventually draw in contributions of more than ***$30 million annually.*** Falwell liked to say that the program was more widely distributed than the Johnny *Carson* Show.

The
OLD-TIME
GOSPEL HOUR
WITH
JERRY FALWELL

In 1979 he founded the ***Moral Majority,*** as a lobbying, educational, and ***political-action committee,*** and served as its president. In his autobiography, Falwell wrote that he "was convinced that there was a ***'moral majority'*** out there...sufficient in number to turn back the flood tide of ***moral permissiveness, family breakdown*** and general ***capitulation to evil*** and to ***foreign policies*** such as Marxism-Leninism."

MORAL MAJORITY

The Moral Majority was a prominent voice of the ***Christian Right*** and campaigned against ***abortion rights, gay rights,*** and the ***Equal Rights Amendment.***

Within ***three years,*** Falwell proudly claimed that the Moral Majority "had a $10 million budget, 100,000 trained pastors, priests, and rabbis, and several million volunteers. And in the process, we helped elect" ***President Ronald Reagan.***

Falwell would testify that in a *Good Housekeeping* magazine poll, he had been named the ***"second most-admired American behind the President,"*** and that *U.S. News and World Report* had included him ***"among the twenty-five most influential Americans."***
However, Falwell's ***kindly telegenic presence*** was often in apparent ***conflict*** with his fiery and ***divisive rhetoric.***

In 1965, he criticized ***Dr. King*** and the Civil Rights Movement as having "done more to ***damage race relations*** and to ***engender hate*** than to help!"

He later repudiated the sermon, but in 1985 he called ***Bishop Desmond M. Tutu,*** the Nobel Peace Prize winner, a "phony," and supported the ***apartheid government.***

He declared that "AIDS is not just ***God's punishment*** for ***homosexuals,*** it is God's punishment for the society that tolerates homosexuals."

Falwell supported ***Israel,*** but said he knew why people "don't like ***Jews...*** [They] can make ***more money*** accidentally than you can on purpose."

He called feminism "a ***satanic attack*** on the home."

And perhaps Falwell's ***most*** inflammatory comment came shortly after ***9/11,*** when he initially cast ***blame*** for the attacks on a coalition of ***liberal groups:*** "I really believe that the ***pagans,*** and the ***abortionists,*** and the ***feminists,*** and the ***gays*** and the ***lesbians*** who are actively trying to make that an alternative lifestyle, the ***ACLU...*** all of them who have tried to ***secularize America,*** I point the finger in their face and say ***'you helped this happen.'"***

No matter how his remarks were received by the general public, Falwell continued to willingly *embrace* his role as a lightning rod for his ***fundamentalist faith.*** In everything Falwell said and did, he set himself out as a ***moral exemplar,*** preaching what he believed were the old-fashioned values necessary to ***save*** America from ***spiritual ruin.***

Meanwhile, ***Larry Flynt,*** the pornography publishing titan, did not necessarily see himself as so ***different*** from Jerry Falwell. Years after their litigation had ended, Flynt reflected:

The truth is, the reverend and I had a lot in common. He was from Virginia, and I was from Kentucky. His father had been a bootlegger, and I had been one too in my 20s before I went into the Navy.

In his late twenties, Flynt continued hustling as a small business owner on the fringes of the law, eventually establishing a string of go-go dancing ***Hustler Clubs*** across Ohio in the early 1970s.

The Hustler
COCKTAIL LOUNGE
HUSTLER

Initially started as a ***newsletter*** to promote his clubs, the first issue of *Hustler* magazine was published in July 1974.

Flynt saw his vision for the magazine in stark ***contrast*** to the established *Playboy* and *Penthouse*, saying he "wanted a sex magazine free of pretense and full of ***fantasy, fiction, satire*** and ***biting humor.*** I wanted to offend ***everyone*** on an equal-opportunity basis."

He demonstrated his keen self-described ***"hillbilly instincts"*** for what would sell magazines by purchasing nude photos of ***Jacqueline Kennedy Onassis*** sunbathing in Greece (from a paparazzo who had been turned down by *Playboy* and *Penthouse*). *Hustler's* August 1975 issue featured full-page ***naked pictures*** of the widowed former First Lady, and quickly sold ***a million copies*** while gaining ***international publicity*** in the mainstream media.

The Wall Street Journal reported that Flynt's formula of "girlie photos that beg the description 'sexually explicit,' and cartoons and stories...that used to circulate only surreptitiously," resulted in "not only the fastest-growing men's magazine around but one of the fastest-growing magazines of any kind, ***ever.***"

SALES

Hustler was an enormous **financial success,** but the magazine's exploding public presence also made it a bigger **target.** Flynt would soon be drawn into a string of trials for **obscenity.**

While fighting obscenity charges in Georgia on March 6, 1978, Flynt and one of his attorneys were walking toward the "slightly shabby but still dignified" courthouse in the town square, when they were **shot multiple times.**

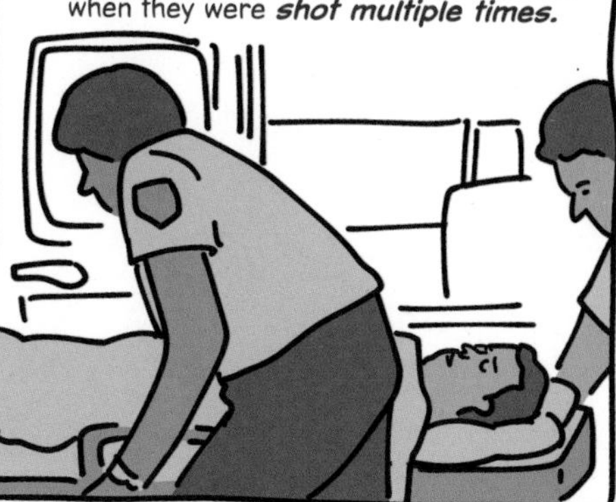

Flynt and the attorney survived. But Flynt would be left **paralyzed** from the waist down and suffering from "peripheral nerve damage" that would cause him **intense pain** for years.

Years later, a **white supremacist** convicted of eight murders, who claimed responsibility for killing another twenty African Americans and Jews between 1977 and 1980, also **confessed** to shooting Flynt. The gunman said he targeted Flynt because he saw photographs in *Hustler's* December 1975 issue of an **interracial couple** having sex.

990133
4 12 05 MO DOC

The incredibly dramatic **twists** and **turns** of Larry Flynt's life would provide the basis for a Golden Globe–winning and Academy Award–nominated film called *The People vs. Larry Flynt* by acclaimed director Milos Forman in 1996 (the latter portion of the biopic dramatizes Flynt's legal fight with Falwell). The "redemption of Larry Flynt" as a free speech **hero** on the screen would be **vigorously challenged** by a number of feminists and First Amendment scholars.

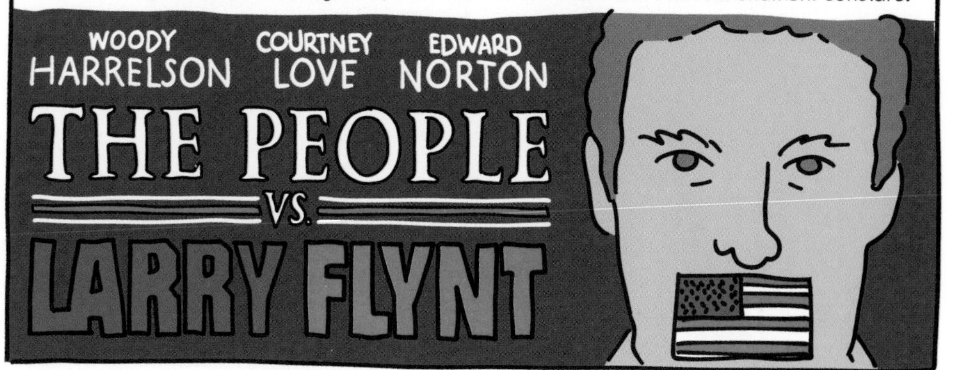
WOODY HARRELSON
COURTNEY LOVE
EDWARD NORTON
THE PEOPLE VS. LARRY FLYNT

One critic points out that in the movie, "we do see the ***notorious*** *Hustler* cover of a naked woman being fed into a ***meat grinder...*** But we ***don't*** see another *Hustler* classic: the picture of a nude woman ***bagged like a deer*** and bound to the ***luggage rack*** of a car."

HUSTLER

"Characterizing Larry Flynt's magazine as sexually ***explicit,*** rather than sexually ***violent,*** reflects a position," maintained Harvard professor **Frederick Schauer.** He advocated that the public should "resist thinking of Larry Flynt's glorification of violence against ***women*** as of a lesser order than the glorification of ***racial*** or ***religious*** violence."

Filmgoers don't see such *Hustler* features as ***"Dirty Pool,"*** which in January 1983 depicted a woman being gang-raped on a pool table...
...[or] such typical *Hustler* photo stories as a naked woman in handcuffs who is shaved, raped and apparently killed by guards in a concentration-camp-like setting.
So, no, I am ***not*** grateful to Mr. Flynt for ***protecting*** my ***freedom,*** as the film and its enthusiasts suggest I should be, no more than I would be to a ***racist*** or ***fascist publisher*** whose speech is protected by the Constitution.

Gloria Steinem, in an op-ed for *The New York Times*

Falwell and Flynt would ***face off*** at trial in Roanoke, Virginia, only forty-five miles from the headquarters of Falwell's religious empire. The lawyers for both sides were an equally pronounced contrast in styles.

Norman Grutman, a highly pedigreed New York trial attorney, represented Falwell. Described as having a deep voice, round body, and boundless self-confidence, he took a pointedly aggressive approach to his dealings with Flynt in the courtroom.

Alan Isaacman, a Beverly Hills litigator with a youthful appearance, presented his case with "an informal, unpretentious style...and a ***slight grin*** on his face."

Isaacman and Flynt became ***good friends.*** Isaacman has said that one of Flynt's lines in the film—"I'm your dream client. I'm the most fun. I'm ***rich.*** And I'm ***always in trouble.***"—was based on how the lawyer described their relationship to colleagues when asked how he could represent the notorious pornographer.

Falwell brought ***two*** main claims against Flynt: ***libel*** and ***intentional infliction of emotional distress.*** The essential distinction between the two legal actions is that libel requires a ***false statement of fact*** and emotional distress does ***not.***

In other words, to ***win*** a libel action, you need to prove that there was a ***factual statement*** that was ***inaccurate,*** not an ***opinion*** statement.
FACT

"Lady *Gaga* hasn't won a *Grammy*" is a ***false statement of fact***—she's actually won more than ***ten.***

"Lady *Gaga* isn't a good singer" is a statement of ***opinion,*** in that it's not provably ***false.***

To win on an emotional distress claim, Falwell needed only to convince a jury that Flynt "intended to inflict emotional distress, was outrageous, and did in fact inflict serious emotional" injury.

As the trial began on December 3, 1984, Grutman led Falwell through questions intended to demonstrate the falsity of the ad. Falwell told the court, "Since I became a Christian in 1952, I have been and am a teetotaler" and never endorsed alcoholic beverages or partook of them before services or at any time.

He testified that his late mother "was a very godly woman, probably the closest to a saint that I have ever known," and that he "would stake [his] life on her purity."

Despite Isaacman's efforts to skip over this impassioned line of questioning, Grutman was allowed by the judge to ask, "Mr. Falwell, specifically, did you and your mother ever commit incest?"

As the jury watched and listened, the discomfort of even having to answer such a question was successfully brought home, and Falwell answered emphatically, "Absolutely not."

Have you attempted to influence public opinion against pornography?
With every breath in my body.

In opposing pornography as a philosophical idea, have either you or the Moral Majority ever personally picked on the intimate personal life of any person who was himself in your judgment a pornographer?"

Never at any time. I don't know anything about the personal lives of the people I consider to be the porn kings.

The ***emotional peak*** of Falwell's testimony came when Grutman sought to draw out the extent of the emotional ***distress*** that the reverend alleged to have suffered. It was an ***indispensable component*** of his claim and something of an awkward fit for the personally ***reserved*** Falwell. He nevertheless rose to the challenge when Grutman asked him for his "personal reaction when [he] read this ad…for the ***first time.***"

I think I have never been as angry as I was at that moment. My first impression was that Campari had purchased an ad in the magazine, because I had seen a similar ad in decent magazines earlier, and my first thought was to get on the phone to Campari. Our in-house attorney and I talked it over. My anger became a more rational and deep hurt.
I somehow felt that in all of my life I had never believed that human beings could do something like this. I really felt like weeping. I am not a deeply emotional person; I don't show it. I think I felt like weeping. It is the most hurtful, damaging, despicable, low-type personal attack that I can imagine one human being can inflict upon another.

It would be ***difficult*** for Larry Flynt to cut as convincing a figure as the apparently ***deeply wounded*** Falwell. However, Flynt rolled into the courtroom in his ***gold-plated wheelchair*** ready to be a polished version of his ***authentic*** and surprisingly ***charming self.***
Isaacman wanted to provide a ***context*** for the Falwell parody ad by having Flynt talk about ***other*** advertising parodies his magazine had created.

Flynt described one *Hustler* parody of Marlboro cigarettes involving...
A ***Marlboro man*** in the hay with his ***horse,*** you know, having ***a cigarette,*** you know, after ***sex...***just a sort of a ***preposterous*** situation.

Isaacman then asked Flynt what was "intended to be ***conveyed***" by this particular Campari ad parody featuring Falwell.

Well, we wanted to poke fun at ***Campari*** for their advertisement because the ***innuendoes*** that they had in their ads made you sort of ***confused*** as to if the person was talking about their ***first time*** as far as a ***sexual encounter*** or whether they were talking about their first time as far as ***drinking Campari.*** Of course, another thing that you had to do is to have a person, you know, that is the ***complete opposite*** of what you would ***expect.***

Jill St. John
about her first

If someone such as *me* might have been in there I don't know *how* people would have interpreted it. But if somebody like *Reverend Falwell* is in there it is very *obvious* that he wouldn't do any of these things; that they are *not true;* that it's not to be taken *seriously.*

...When somebody asks me *why Reverend Falwell,* the only thing I can point out is why did *Walter Mondale,* during the debates in Louisville [ask], "Do you want Reverend Falwell to be involved in selecting the next *Supreme Court?"* Now, that was strictly to make a political point, but that means that *he,* more than *any other evangelist,* is involved in the *mainstream* of politics.

And there is a great deal of people in this country, *especially* the ones that read *Hustler* magazine, that feel that there should be a *separation* between *church and state.*

So, when something like *this* appears it will give people a *chuckle.* They *know* this was not intended to *defame* the Reverend Falwell, his mother or any members of his family because *no one* could take it *serious.*

Isaacman inquired next about the ***"believability"*** of what was written in the ad parody.

Well, you know, as far as making it with ***his mother,*** I mean, that's so ***outrageous,*** I mean, that no one can find that believable. I mean, someone may not ***like it,*** but that's not what we're here for today is whether somebody likes it or not, but whether it's in violation of ***the law.***
FALWELL: I never really expected to make it with Mom, but then after she showed all the other guys in town such a good time, I figured, "What the hell!"
INTERVIEWER: But your mom? Isn't that a bit odd?
FALWELL: I don't think so. Looks don't mean that much to me in a woman.

Finally, Isaacman questioned Flynt as to whether his intent with the ad parody was to harm Falwell.

I don't have any, you know, ***personal*** animosity...towards Reverend Falwell. I put him, you know, like ***all politicians*** and ***all evangelists,*** basically in the ***same category.*** *Hustler* ***satirizes*** and ***parodies,*** and our basic editorial content is built around ***politics, sex*** and ***religion.***
HUSTLER
Special Political Issue
THE TEN WORST CONGRESSMEN
WHITE HOUSE SEX SCANDALS
THE BIZARRE POLITICS OF LYNDON LAROU
HUSTLER

Flynt had accomplished all they could hope to with his testimony, making his position clear: The mockery was ***not*** intended to be taken ***personally,*** and the extreme nature of the falsehoods was the ***very reason*** the parody could not reasonably harm Falwell's ***reputation*** or ***feelings.***

At closing argument, the local paper reported that Grutman, in a rising voice, sought to "make a statement about what he saw as the ***sleaze*** running wild in America."

Certainly the ***eyes of the country*** are on Roanoke. And you are going to make ***a statement.***
And that statement that you are going to make from this courthouse is going to ***spread*** throughout the ***length and breadth*** of this land.
The ***nation*** is watching. The nation wants to know where the Constitution stands. ***Which way,*** America? Are you going to let loose ***chaos*** and ***anarchy?*** Are you going to turn America into the ***Planet of the Apes?***

Isaacman, in contrast, summed it up as a ***narrow*** First Amendment question.
It would be ***ridiculous*** [to award damages] on the basis of something as frivolous as ***hurt feelings.***

After the weeklong trial, the all-white, all-Protestant jury of four men and eight women from the Bible Belt deliberated for about ***six hours*** before returning their verdict.
They found that the ad parody could ***not*** "reasonably be understood as describing ***actual facts*** about [Falwell] or actual ***events*** in which [he] participated," and that as a result, Flynt ***did not*** libel Falwell.
The jury then ruled for Falwell on the emotional distress claim, and awarded him $200,000 in damages. The split decision, and the relatively modest damages, meant both sides would claim victory—
—and ***both*** sides would ***appeal*** parts of the decision.

UNITED STATES COURT OF APPEALS
FOR THE FOURTH CIRCUIT

Almost two years later, the Fourth Circuit ***affirmed*** the judgment, rejecting Flynt's arguments that the emotional distress claim was limited by the First Amendment. For the first time, a federal court of appeals held that a public figure could recover damages for emotional distress ***without*** a finding of libel or invasion of privacy.

Yet, Flynt and Isaacman ***pressed on,*** and the case proved to be such a ***novel*** and ***significant*** free speech issue that the high court agreed to hear it.

Isaacman began by arguing that the actual malice standard set out in ***Sullivan*** to protect libel defendants should not be ***"evaded*** by a ***public figure...***by labeling his cause of action intentional infliction of emotional distress" instead.

Justice Sandra Day O'Connor asked if the state has "an even ***greater*** interest" in protecting its citizens from ***emotional distress*** than it does in protecting ***reputation.***

Isaacman deftly replied that ***reputational injury*** should be considered ***more important,*** since it impacts "what goes on in the minds of ***other*** people as well, and not just the minds of ***one citizen."*** Isaacman was purposefully laying the foundation for his position that the actual malice standard should apply to ***both emotional distress*** as well as ***libel claims.***

Justice Byron White queried if Isaacman believed that "opinion or parody is **never** actionable," to which he responded that parody should **always be protected** as long as it is concerns **public figures** and "contains nothing that can be understood as a **false statement of fact.**"

PARODY

Justice John Paul Stevens then asked what the public interest in parody **was.** Isaacman seemed well prepared for this line of inquiry.

He explained that the **first** interest arises when "somebody who's out there campaigning against it saying don't read our magazine and we're **poison** on the minds of America and **don't engage in sex** outside of **wedlock** and **don't drink alcohol.** *Hustler* has **every right** to say that man is full of **B.S.** And that's what this ad parody says."

The **second** interest was in putting Falwell "in a ridiculous setting. Instead of Jerry Falwell speaking from the television with a **beatific** look on his face and the **warmth** that comes out of him, and the **sincerity** in his voice...and he's standing on a pulpit, and he may have a bible in his hand...*Hustler* is saying, let's **deflate** this **stuffed shirt,** let's bring him **down** to **our level...**or at **least** to the level where you will listen to what **we** have to say."

The rule you give us says that if you stand for public office, or become a public figure in any way, you cannot protect yourself, or indeed, your mother, against a parody of your committing incest with your mother in an outhouse.
Justice Antonin Scalia

What you're talking about, Justice Scalia, is a matter of taste. And as...you said [in a previous decision], just as it's useless to argue about taste, it's useless to litigate it.

How often do you think you're going to be able to get a jury to find that [the parody] was done with the intent of creating emotional distress?

Every time.

Almost every time that something ***critical*** is said about somebody, because how can any speaker come in and say ***I didn't intend to cause any emotional distress,*** and be ***believed.*** If you say something critical about another person, and if it's ***very critical,*** it's ***going*** to cause ***emotional distress.***

That's ***why*** that's a ***meaningless standard.***

It was an ***auspicious*** way to conclude, and as Isaacman sat down, he ***winked*** at Flynt.

Grutman started his argument off with ***strong words:***
Deliberate, malicious ***character assassination*** is ***not protected*** by the Constitution. Deliberate, malicious character assassination is what was ***proven*** in this case.

Calling Flynt's conduct ***"aberrational,"*** Grutman tried to assure the Court that other ***"responsible" publishers*** need not worry about any ***precedent*** in this case. He emphatically stated that "this is the wanton, reckless, deliberately malicious publisher who sets out for the sheer ***perverse joy*** of simply causing injury to abuse the power that he has as a publisher."

But Justice O'Connor was clearly not convinced that a ***victory*** for Falwell could be ***contained,*** asking, "Do you think a ***vicious cartoon*** should subject the drawer of that cartoon to ***potential liability?"***
Grutman refused to put any limits on emotional distress claims, other than saying a jury would determine if a cartoon "would be regarded by the average member of the community as so intolerable that no civilized person should have to bear it."
It was a definite ***tactical error,*** which Justice White commented on with some dismay:
Well, Mr. Grutman, you're certainly posing a much ***broader proposition*** than is ***necessary*** for you to win this case.

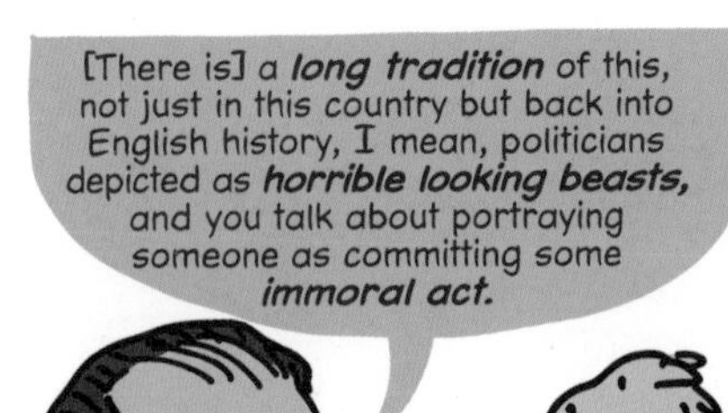
[There is] a *long tradition* of this, not just in this country but back into English history, I mean, politicians depicted as *horrible looking beasts,* and you talk about portraying someone as committing some *immoral act.*
I would be *very* surprised if there were not a number of cartoons depicting one or another *political figure* as at least the piano player in a *bordello.*
MONOPOLY
VOTE
$
Grutman tried to *play along.*
We don't *shoot* the *piano player.* I understand that.

Give us *something* that the *cartoonist* or the *political figure* can *adhere to.* I mean, does it depend on how *ugly* the beast is, or *what?*
COTTON
I believe that this is a matter of an *evolving social* sensibility.
By saying this, Grutman meant simply: *Juries* could sort it out.

In today's world, people don't *want* to have to take these things to a *jury.* They want to have some kind of a *rule* to follow, so that when they *utter it* or *write it* or *draw it* in the first place, they're *comfortable* in the knowledge that it *isn't* going to subject them to a *suit.*

Grutman only offered that a "responsible author, artist, or anyone" would *somehow know.*

Even the supremely *self-assured* Grutman must have realized his argument was *not* winning over the justices.

Almost three months later, on February 24, 1988, Larry Flynt answered a phone call at his office.
Larry, I've got some incredible news—*we won!* It was a unanimous decision.
The unlikely victory also had an unlikely author. *Chief Justice William Rehnquist,* who at that time was viewed as *"anti-press,"* wrote the decision for the Court.
Seeking to frame the opinion in *expansive terms,* the chief justice began by citing *past precedent.*
One of the *prerogatives* of American citizenship is the *right to criticize public men and measures.* Such criticism, *inevitably,* will not always be reasoned or moderate; public figures...will be subject to *vehement, caustic,* and sometimes unpleasantly *sharp attacks.*
FACT
PARODY
The First Amendment question before the Court, he succinctly set forth, was "whether a public figure may recover damages for emotional harm caused by the publication of an ad parody *offensive to him...*and [that] is *intended* to inflict *emotional injury,* even when that speech could not *reasonably* have been interpreted as stating *actual facts* about the public figure involved."
The answer must be *no,* Rehnquist wrote, unless a jury finds that "the publication contains a *false statement of fact* which was made with *'actual malice,'* i.e., with *knowledge* that the statement was false or with *reckless disregard* as to whether or not it was true."

Applying ***New York Times v. Sullivan,*** actual malice safeguards were necessary, he added, "to give adequate ***'breathing space'*** to the freedoms protected by the First Amendment."

NYT v. SULLIVAN

Rehnquist explained that protecting such parody was absolutely ***necessary*** because "were we to hold otherwise, there can be little doubt that ***political cartoonists*** and ***satirists*** would be subjected to damages awards ***without any showing*** that their work falsely defamed its subject."

Looking back on ***Thomas Nast*** cartoons attacking the corruption of New York City's ***"Boss" Tweed,*** he quoted experts who pointed out such art succeeded in its day through "the ***emotional impact*** of its ***presentation*** [that] continuously goes beyond the bounds of ***good taste*** and ***conventional manners.***"

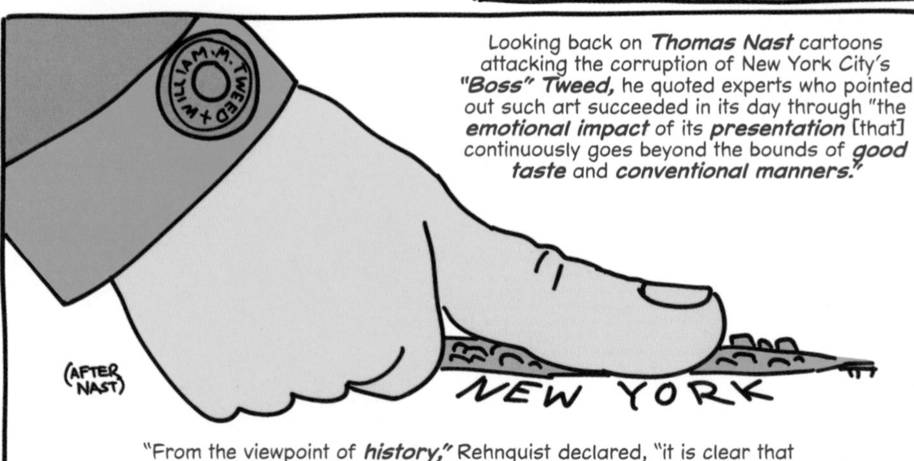
WILLIAM M. TWEED
(AFTER NAST)
NEW YORK

"From the viewpoint of ***history,"*** Rehnquist declared, "it is clear that our ***political discourse*** would have been considerably ***poorer*** without them."

There is ***no doubt*** that the caricature of [Falwell] and his mother published in *Hustler* is ***at best*** a ***distant cousin*** of the political cartoons described above, and a rather ***poor*** relation at that.

Jerry Falwell talks about his first time.*

If it were possible...to separate the ***one*** from ***the other,*** public discourse would probably suffer little or no harm. But we doubt that there is any such standard, and...the pejorative description ***"outrageous"*** does not supply one. "Outrageousness" in the area of political and social discourse has an inherent ***subjectiveness...***which would allow a jury to impose liability on the basis of the jurors' ***tastes or views,*** or perhaps... their ***dislike*** of a ***particular expression.***

The decision was as impactful as it was ***surprising.*** Public figures simply cannot recover for even the most ***outrageous, unbelievable satiric attacks,*** despite the fact that there may be an ***intent*** to cause ***emotional harm.***
It also reaffirmed the ***Sullivan*** decision, and its free speech protections of the press from lawsuits brought by public figures, as a ***bedrock principle*** of the First Amendment.
And in preserving the free speech rights of someone as ***tawdry*** as Flynt, the Court demonstrated that the First Amendment cloaks ***all of us*** in its embrace.
Heed Their Rising Voices

As Chief Justice Rehnquist rhapsodized in his decision, "At the ***heart*** of the First Amendment is the recognition of the fundamental importance of the ***free flow of ideas*** and opinions on matters of public interest and concern.

Ideas

"The freedom to ***speak one's mind*** is not only an aspect of ***individual liberty***—and thus a good unto itself—but also is ***essential*** to the common quest for ***truth*** and the ***vitality*** of society as a whole."

For Flynt and Falwell, the far-reaching decision would eventually lead to a ***strange new chapter*** in their contentious relationship. Immediately after the Supreme Court announced their ruling, the pair traded ***predictable insults.***
But almost ten years later, with the opening of *The People vs. Larry Flynt* and the release of Flynt's autobiography, both men appeared together on CNN's *Larry King Live* and Falwell ***hugged*** Flynt!

Soon after, Falwell came to Flynt's office to propose the two "go around the country debating... moral issues and First Amendment issues."
Over the course of this college tour, and in the years that followed, the two visited with each other and developed a relationship.

Jerry Falwell once made a remark that I didn't save the First Amendment, the First Amendment saved me. And I said "Jerry, that's the first thing you've ever said that I ***agree with.***"

A few days after Falwell's death in 2007, Flynt wrote in the *Los Angeles Times* that "the ultimate result was one I never expected and was just as shocking a turn to me as was winning that famous Supreme Court case: We became ***friends.***"

Whether Trump will ever feel equally ***friendly*** toward *Saturday Night Live* is impossible to predict.
What is known because of ***Hustler v. Falwell*** is that there is ***nothing*** Trump can legally do to stop the satire. No matter how ***outrageous,*** no matter how filled with ***animus,*** no matter how ***hurt*** the feelings. ***Mockery, caricature,*** and ***ridicule*** are the price that all public figures ***pay*** to keep America's most outlandish ideas ***freely flowing.***

Chapter 9:

NAZIS IN CHARLOTTESVILLE, FUNERAL PROTESTS, AND SPEAKERS WE HATE

In the darkness of night, punctuated by the fiery glow of tiki torches, the angry chants rang out...

You will not replace us!
Jews will not replace us!
Blood and soil!
White lives matter!

More than ***300 white nationalists*** were marching in an unannounced processional on the campus of the ***University of Virginia.*** They were just some of the self-identified ***neo-Nazis, Ku Klux Klan*** (KKK) members, and other ***alt-right*** adherents who had come to ***Charlottesville*** for a ***"Unite the Right"*** rally scheduled to take place the ***next day.***

The rally had been organized by ***Jason Kessler,*** a local resident and University of Virginia graduate who described himself as a ***"white advocate."*** On his permit application, Kessler described the event as a ***"free speech rally"*** for an estimated 400 participants at ***Emancipation Park.***

The initial purpose for the rally was to oppose the city council's efforts to ***remove*** a statue of the Confederate general ***Robert E. Lee*** from that park, which, until three months prior, had been named after Lee.

However, in a later interview, Kessler said his goal for Unite the Right was to "***destigmatize*** white advocacy so that white people can stand up for their interests just like any other identity group."

Five days before the rally, city officials informed Kessler that they would only grant a permit to hold the event at a ***larger park,*** based on information that "many thousands of individuals are likely to attend the demonstration," and that officials "cannot adequately ***protect people*** and ***property*** in and around Emancipation Park."
CITY HALL

The Virginia ***ACLU*** took up Kessler's case, arguing that the city's reasons for denying the permit at the park of Kessler's choice were only a "***pretext*** for silencing the 'Unite the Right' demonstration."
ACLU

The Judge ruled for Kessler, having determined that the "decision to revoke Kessler's permit was based on the ***content of his speech*** rather than other neutral factors."

On the morning of August 12, 2017, the largest gathering of white nationalists in ***decades*** was heading toward Emancipation Park.

RACIST ZONE

Violence soon broke out between the ***alt-right*** and ***counterprotesters*** as police stood by unable or unwilling to do anything to stop it.

As the fighting grew more ***intense,*** about a half an hour before the rally was officially set to begin at noon, the Charlottesville Police Chief declared the event an ***"unlawful assembly."***

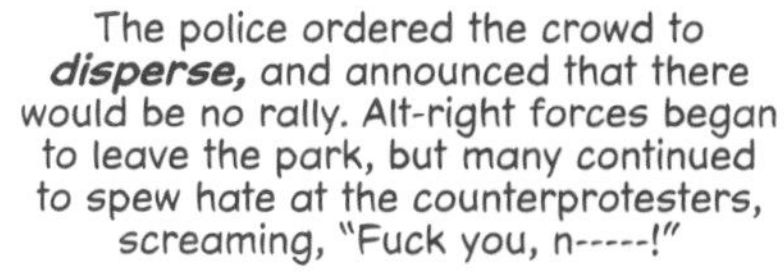

The police ordered the crowd to ***disperse,*** and announced that there would be no rally. Alt-right forces began to leave the park, but many continued to spew hate at the counterprotesters, screaming, "Fuck you, n-----!"

The unintended result of the police action was that the fighting ***spread*** beyond the park as "small groups of people wandered through the streets and engaged in frequent ***skirmishes*** unimpeded by police."

Almost two hours after the rally was canceled, a Unite the Right participant drove his gray Dodge Challenger up to a narrow street crowded with counterprotesters and then ***intentionally*** accelerated, ramming his car into them.

One witness described hearing "this sound of...***hitting,*** like traffic cones. This hollow, ***horrible sound."*** The driver then ***reversed*** quickly, ***hitting*** and ***dragging*** others. Dozens were injured in the attack and thirty-two-year-old ***Heather Heyer*** was ***killed*** at the scene.

Heyer was a Charlottesville resident and worked as a paralegal at a local law firm. She was attending the rally with friends as an ***anti-racism*** demonstrator, and had been chanting, ***"Whose streets? Our streets!"*** shortly before she was murdered.

President Trump added fuel to the fire when, later that day, he responded to the tragic events: "We condemn in the strongest possible terms this egregious display of hatred, bigotry and violence ***on many sides,"*** adding again for emphasis with a wave of his hand, ***"On many sides."***

Equating neo-Nazis, the KKK, and white supremacists with those ***protesting*** racism triggered a ***widespread outcry,*** even from prominent members of his ***own party.***

And so under ***pressure,*** Trump reluctantly offered an actual condemnation of racism and hate groups. But another day later, he ***doubled down*** on his previous remarks, insisting "you had some very bad people in that group, but you also had people that were ***very fine people,*** on ***both sides."***

Charlottesville mayor ***Mike Signer*** responded strongly, "I'm not going to make any bones about it. I place the ***blame*** for a lot of what you're seeing in America today right at the doorstep of the ***White House*** and the people around ***the president."***

Whatever may have caused or exacerbated this ***hate,*** the tragedy of Charlottesville and Trump's response had certainly highlighted the festering forces of ***white nationalism*** that still exist in this country.

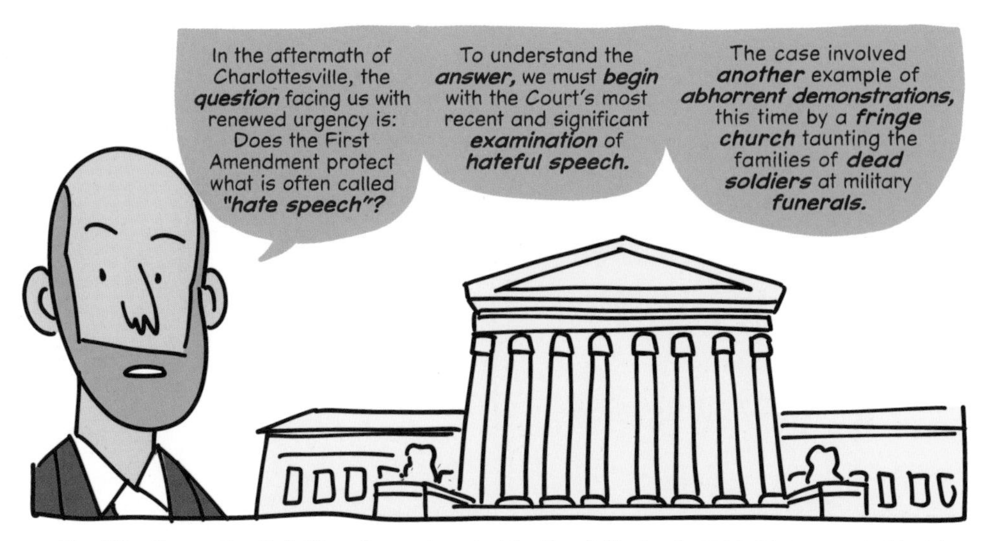
In the aftermath of Charlottesville, the *question* facing us with renewed urgency is: Does the First Amendment protect what is often called *"hate speech"*?
To understand the *answer,* we must *begin* with the Court's most recent and significant *examination* of *hateful speech.*
The case involved *another* example of *abhorrent demonstrations,* this time by a *fringe church* taunting the families of *dead soldiers* at military *funerals.*

The ***Westboro Baptist Church*** was founded by ***Fred Phelps*** in 1955. Phelps made his living as a successful ***civil rights lawyer*** in Topeka, Kansas, representing African Americans in ***discrimination lawsuits,*** until he was disbarred for ***unethical behavior*** in 1979.

The church's small congregation was made up primarily of members of his family. He and his wife, Margie, had thirteen children, fifty-four grandchildren, and seven great-grandchildren, who mostly lived together in a compound of houses they called "the Block."

WBC
WESTBORO BAPTIST CHURCH

In the 1990s, Westboro started in on its ***anti-gay crusade*** and gained attention for protesting against homosexuality at the ***funerals*** of people who had died of AIDS.

FAGS
ARE
FREAKS
OF
NATURE

Picketing at the funeral of ***Matthew Shepard,*** the twenty-one-year-old gay college student who was ***beaten to death*** in Laramie, Wyoming, garnered the church ***national exposure.***

The messages on their signs showed the world what would become the church's recognizably ***signature*** combination of ***hate*** and ***appalling personal attacks.***

MATT
IN
HELL
GOD
HATES
FAGS

In 2001, Phelps attested that ***9/11*** was ***God's punishment*** for America's ***acceptance*** of homosexuality.

THANK
GOD
FOR
9/11

In 2005, Westboro started picketing at the funerals of ***armed forces personnel*** killed in Iraq and Afghanistan. Phelps's ***convoluted*** rationale for this new outrage was that ***God*** wanted those troops dead as a sign to ***warn Americans*** of the error of their ways.

PRAY
FOR
MORE
DEAD
SOLDIERS
SOLDIERS
DIE
GOD
LAUGHS

The Westboro Baptist Church picketed at ***hundreds*** of funerals and almost certainly added to the ***trauma*** experienced by the grieving families at one of the most ***vulnerable*** and ***painful*** times in their lives.

Of all the people impacted, the ***father*** of one of those veterans decided to ***take action.*** His fight would lead him on a five-year journey attempting to change the path of ***hate speech*** and First Amendment law.

HATE
Albert Snyder

Matt Snyder was a senior in high school when he told his father, Albert, that he wanted to join the military. Albert said he would ***support*** his son's choice, but asked Matt to take "a couple of weeks to really ***think*** about this," since the ***war*** in ***Iraq*** was "not getting any better."

Matt decided to join the ***Marines,*** and in 2005 during a Christmas visit home, he told his family he was being ***deployed*** to Iraq.

On March 3, 2006, after being in Iraq for only a few weeks, Matt was on a mission in Al Anbar Province when he was ***killed*** in the line of duty. He was only twenty years old.

A week later, the funeral for Lance Corporal Matthew Snyder was held at their family's Catholic church, St. John's, in Westminster, Maryland. Albert was deeply moved to see ***thousands*** of people on the streets paying tribute to Matt.

WE

Albert noticed that their driver took the ***service entrance*** to bring them around to the church. At the time, Albert didn't know why they had gone that way, but the ***reason*** soon became clear: ***Fred Phelps,*** along with two of his daughters and four of his grandchildren, had flown in from Kansas to ***picket*** Snyder's funeral. Following police instructions, they were standing behind orange snow fencing, about 1,000 feet away from the church.

GOD HATES THE U.S.
POPE IN HELL
PRIESTS
THANK GOD FOR IEDs
GOD HATES FAGS .COM
THANK GOD FOR DEAD SOLDIERS

Albert Snyder could only see the tops of the signs, but not ***what they said,*** from the limo. Shortly after the funeral services began in the church, the Phelps family packed up their signs and left.

At the wake later that day, the family turned on the television, and ***that*** is when Albert first saw ***the signs.*** What the Church didn't know is that, although Matt was heterosexual, Albert is gay. His friends and family knew, but his sexual orientation was otherwise a ***private matter.***

GOD HATES THE U.S.
POPE IN HELL
PRIESTS

Many years later, Albert remembered how his loved ones "hated to see ***me*** and my ***partner*** and my ***friends*** have to deal with something ***so vicious*** at a funeral," adding sorrowfully, "I had ***one*** opportunity to ***bury my son,*** and it was ***taken away*** from me. He should have had a ***peaceful burial.***"

Albert Snyder decided to ***sue*** Phelps and the Westboro Baptist Church in federal court for ***intentional infliction of emotional distress*** and other claims.

After a ten-day trial, The jury found in favor of ***Snyder*** and awarded him ***$2.9 million*** in compensatory damages and ***$8 million*** in punitive damages.

Although the loss appeared ***devastating,*** Phelp's church posted a video in which members ***jubilantly*** said that they "thank God for the $10.9 million verdict because it's a ***small price*** to pay to get this message—***America is doomed***—in front of the eyes of the whole world. You can't pay for worldwide publicity that ***cheap!***"

Fred Phelps's daughter, ***Margie,*** who, like her father, was a lawyer, filed their appeal and was confident God "would turn our apparent defeat into a ***victory.***"

On appeal, the Fourth Circuit held the First Amendment ***fully protected*** Westboro's speech as involving matters of ***public concern*** (as opposed to ***private matters,*** which are afforded less First Amendment protection).

Judge Robert B. King seemed pained and almost ***apologetic*** to write that "it is a fair summary of history to say that the safeguards of liberty have often been forged in controversies involving ***not very nice people.***"

The Fourth Circuit's ruling was a nearly **fatal blow** to Albert Snyder's quest for justice. He had only **one remaining chance** to try to achieve his goal of holding the Westboro Baptist Church **accountable** for their actions.
To the dismay of **some** court watchers, the Supreme Court opened the door to that possibility when it agreed to hear the **appeal.**

As the oral argument drew near, the **political impact** of the case, beyond just a father's fight, became clearer. **Forty-eight states** and a **bipartisan coalition** of forty-three senators filed briefs **supporting Snyder.** The attorneys general brief advocated that this uniquely **"intrusive and harassing"** speech that amounted to **"emotional terrorism"** could and should be **restricted** without running afoul of the First Amendment.

On the **opposite** side, **news** and **civil liberties organizations** lined up to provide briefs stressing that the **media** and **college campuses** would both feel the chill if the Fourth Circuit decision was not **upheld.** A *New York Times* editorial urged that it was in the nation's interest to ensure "that strong language about large issues be protected, even when it is **hard to do so.**"
The New York Times
ACLU

Outside the Supreme Court on October 6, 2010, the Westboro Baptist Church had once again turned a solemn proceeding into ***circus.*** The church had chosen to ***picket*** outside the building where one of their own faithful members–***Margie Phelps***–was about to argue inside.

THANK GOD FOR DEAD SOLDIERS
GOD HATES YOU
SOLDIERS DIE GOD LAUGHS
THANK GOD FOR 9/11
GOD HATES OBAMA

Counterprotesters responded to the Westboro provocations with humor.

SIGNS ARE SO GAY!
IF YOU'RE GOING TO HEAVEN, HELL SOUNDS NICE

Inside, the limits of ***hateful speech*** were about to be debated in a much less jocular manner. Albert Snyder, his partner Walt Fisher, and Al's daughters and sisters were seated near members of the church.

JEWS KILLED CHRIST

Sean Summers, a Maryland attorney who had been representing Snyder pro bono, started off with his ***strongest point:***

We are talking about ***a funeral.*** If context is ever going to matter, it ***has*** to matter in the context of a funeral. Mr. Snyder simply wanted to bury his son in a ***private, dignified manner.*** [Westboro Baptist Church's] behavior made that ***impossible.***

As a result, according to Summers, Snyder should be allowed to bring an intentional infliction of ***emotional distress*** claim without it being ***blocked*** by the First Amendment. After those few sentences, Summers was on the ***defensive*** for the rest of his argument.

Summers tried to argue that the First Amendment limits on intentional emotional distress claims that prohibited recovery in ***Hustler v. Falwell*** did not apply in this case. He distinguished ***Hustler*** based on the fact that Reverend Falwell was a ***public*** figure and here Snyder was a ***private*** figure.
Hustler seems to me to have one sentence that is ***key*** to the whole decision... It says: "***Outrageousness*** in the area of political and social discourse has an inherent ***subjectiveness*** about it which would allow a jury to impose liability on the basis of the jurors' ***tastes or views*** or perhaps on the basis of their ***dislike*** of a particular expression."
How is that sentence ***less*** implicated in a case about a ***private*** figure than in a case about a ***public*** figure?
Justice Elena Kagan
Summers replied by saying the parody in *Hustler* was a "traditional area of public discourse," as opposed to "a private funeral."
HUSTLER
This seemed to do little to ***assuage*** Kagan's concern about the ***dangers*** inherent in giving juries ***free reign*** to punish ***unpopular speech*** about matters of public interest.
Most of the other justices showed they were also very concerned about how to ***draw a line*** that would allow Snyder to recover without leading to a ***chilling impact*** on too much other speech. Summers seemed cowed and unable to provide any ***substantive First Amendment framework*** that would accommodate Snyder.
Margie Phelps was in for an equally ***rough time*** before the justices and only got one sentence out before she was interrupted with a series of ***hypotheticals.***
Justice Samuel Alito Jr.
Suppose someone believes that African Americans are... ***inherently*** inferior, and they are really a ***bad influence*** on this country. And so [that] person comes up to an African American and starts ***berating*** that person with ***racial hatred...*** That's a matter of ***public*** concern?

Ms. Phelps replied that she thought "the issue of ***race*** is a matter of ***public concern,"*** but that the she also thought "approaching an individual ***up close*** and ***in their grill*** to berate them gets you out of the ***zone of protection,*** and we would never do that."
With much of the discussion centering on ***what*** could be said, ***Justice Ruth Bader Ginsburg*** zeroed in on the issue of ***where*** the picketing should be allowed to occur.
This is a case about ***exploiting*** a private family's ***grief*** and the question is, why should the First Amendment tolerate exploiting this ***Marine's family,*** when you have so many ***other*** forums for getting across your message?
Phelps got hung up objecting to the term ***exploiting.*** It was indicative of her performance throughout, technically ***respectful,*** but intransigent in her repeated ***refusal*** to directly answer many of the questions. Both counsels appeared to have done ***little*** to advance their causes.
After the arguments, Mr. Snyder told the press that he had ***no issue*** with Westboro picketing nearby. "Take it to the Supreme Court, that's what they're supposed to do," he explained. "But 99% of Americans would agree that you can't protest a ***funeral."***
Not surprisingly, church members were acting far ***less reasonably.***
*Cryin' 'bout your feeeeeelings for your sin, no shame! You're goin' straight to Hell on your crazy train!**
Sung to the tune of Ozzy Osbourne's "Crazy Train."

Despite the justices' apparent struggle at oral argument with the facts and devising limits for both sides, the vote was nearly unanimous. The Westboro Baptist Church had prevailed, 8 to 1, with only Justice Alito dissenting.
The majority ruled that the First Amendment protected the church from liability for their speech on a matter of public concern in a public place, which did not actually disrupt or physically interfere with a funeral.
Whether the First Amendment prohibits holding Westboro liable for its speech in this case turns largely on whether that speech is of public or private concern, as determined by all the circumstances of the case.
The First Amendment reflects "a profound national commitment to the principle that debate on public issues should be uninhibited, robust, and wide-open...
"...because speech concerning public affairs is more than self-expression; it is the essence of self-government."
Accordingly, "speech on public issues occupies the highest rung of the hierarchy of First Amendment values, and is entitled to special protection."
Chief Justice John Roberts

The somewhat vague ***guidance*** he then offered is "speech deals with matters of ***public concern*** when it can be fairly considered as relating to any matter of political, social, or other concern to the ***community,*** or when it is a subject of legitimate news interest," adding that the "inappropriate or controversial character of a statement is ***irrelevant.***"

To determine whether Westboro's speech was "of public or private concern," Chief Justice Roberts examined its ***content*** and ***context.***

While these messages may fall short of ***refined*** social or political commentary, the ***issues*** they highlight—the ***political*** and ***moral conduct*** of the United States and its citizens, the ***fate*** of our Nation, homosexuality in the ***military,*** and ***scandals*** involving the Catholic clergy—are matters of ***public import.***

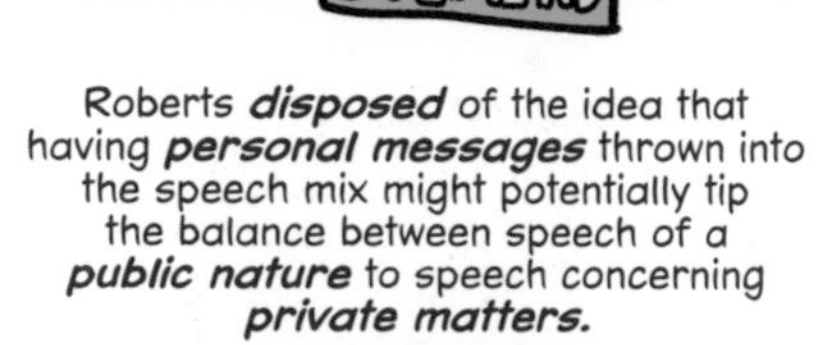
POPE IN HELL
PRAY FOR MORE DEAD SOLDIERS
GOD HATES FAGS

Roberts ***disposed*** of the idea that having ***personal messages*** thrown into the speech mix might potentially tip the balance between speech of a ***public nature*** to speech concerning ***private matters.***

Even if a few of the signs—such as ***"You're Going to Hell"*** and ***"God Hates You"***—were viewed as containing messages related to Matthew Snyder or the Snyders ***specifically,*** that would not change the fact that the overall thrust and ***dominant theme*** of Westboro's demonstration spoke to ***broader*** public issues.

The key then is whether the ***"dominant theme"*** or main point of the speech is about a matter of public concern.
This way, the majority cuts off the problem of courts having to read ***every sign*** at a protest to determine if any might enable ***punishment*** of the speakers.

Reviewing the ***context*** of Westboro's speech, Chief Justice Roberts arrived at the ***funeral*** issue. The fact that Westboro was picketing on a public street meant that despite being ***near*** the funeral, it had located itself squarely in a quintessential ***"public forum,"*** where making space for free speech is traditionally ***most protected*** by the Court.

GO
HAT
TH
U.S.
POPE
IN
HELL
PRIESTS
THANK GOD FOR IEDs
GOD HATES FAGS .COM
THANK GOD FOR DEAD SOLDIERS

The chief justice recognized that even in such a public forum, the state can ***still*** impose ***"reasonable time, place, or manner restrictions"*** on expressive activity, as long as the laws are ***"content neutral"*** (meaning a law that applies the same to all speech no matter what the subject matter or content of the speech may be).

In ***this*** circumstance, however, the damages were imposed entirely ***because of the content*** of the message expressed.

POPE
IN
HELL

For the majority, ***this*** was the ***fatal flaw*** at the heart of the case. The chief justice reminded us that Westboro's "speech ***cannot*** be restricted simply because it is ***upsetting*** or ***arouses contempt.***"

If there is a ***bedrock principle*** underlying the First Amendment, it is that the government may not prohibit the expression of an ***idea*** simply because society finds the idea itself ***offensive*** or ***disagreeable.***

Indeed, the point of all speech protection... is to ***shield*** just those choices of content that in someone's eyes are ***misguided,*** or ***even hurtful.***

PRAY FOR MORE DEAD SOLDIERS
SOLDIERS DIE GOD LAUGHS

Westboro's funeral picketing is certainly hurtful and its contribution to public discourse may be negligible. But Westboro addressed matters of public import on public property, in a peaceful manner, in full compliance with the guidance of local officials.
THANK GOD FOR DEAD SOLDIERS
FAGS ARE FREAKS OF NATURE
SOLDIERS DIE GOD LAUGHS

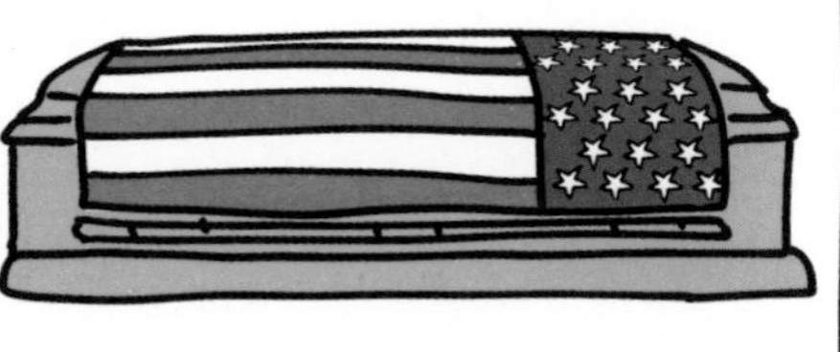
The speech was indeed planned to coincide with Matthew Snyder's funeral, but did not itself disrupt that funeral, and Westboro's choice to conduct its picketing at that time and place did not alter the nature of its speech.

Speech is powerful. It can stir people to action, move them to tears of both joy and sorrow, and—as it did here—inflict great pain. On the facts before us, we cannot react to that pain by punishing the speaker.
As a Nation we have chosen a different course—to protect even hurtful speech on public issues to ensure that we do not stifle public debate.

In these lines, Chief Justice Roberts, a self-described "aggressive defender" of the First Amendment, strongly *reaffirmed* a few fundamental tenets of the Supreme Court's established view of free speech and its *role* in our society.
Robust debate on *public issues* is a *central part* the American experience. Protecting hateful speech is *necessary* to maintain free debate. Therefore, as a trade-off for the *greater good,* some will suffer *great pain* from the speech of *others.*
Justice Alito, in his solitary dissent, responded *contemptuously* to *all* of his fellow justices, and put forth a very *different* interpretation of what the First Amendment requires.
Our *profound* national commitment to free and open debate is not a license for the vicious *verbal assault* that occurred in this case.
Albert Snyder is not a *public figure.* He is simply a *parent...*[who] wanted what is surely the right of *any* parent who experiences such an *incalculable loss:* to bury his son in peace. But...members of the Westboro Baptist Church *deprived* him of that elementary right.
PRAY FOR MORE DEAD SOLDIERS

Alito then challenged the majority on ***two points*** underlying their decision. ***First,*** he described why in his view the church went "far ***beyond commentary*** on matters of ***public concern,"*** and in fact had ***"specifically attacked Matthew Snyder*** because (1) he was a ***Catholic*** and (2) he was a member of the ***United States military."***

POPE IN HELL
PRAY FOR MORE DEAD SOLDIERS
THANK GOD FOR IEDs

In his opinion, this "attack on Matthew was of ***central importance"*** to Westboro's speech.

And Alito contended that even if he were to accept the majority's finding that "the ***overall thrust*** and ***dominant theme*** of [their] demonstration spoke to broad public issues," he did not agree that ***"actionable speech*** should be immunized simply because it is interspersed with speech that is ***protected."***

PUBLIC
PRIVATE

Second, Justice Alito criticized the majority for ***overvaluing*** the fact that the picketing occurred on a public street.
There is ***no reason*** why a public street in close proximity to the scene of a ***funeral*** should be regarded as a ***free-fire zone*** in which otherwise ***actionable*** verbal attacks are shielded from liability.

In an endnote to the majority opinion, Justice Roberts addressed this line of the dissent.

The fact that Westboro conducted its picketing adjacent to a public street does ***not*** insulate the speech from liability, but instead ***heightens concerns*** that what is at issue is an effort to communicate to the public the church's views on matters of public concern.

Alito finished by focusing on the ***brutality*** of speech and the feelings of the grieving family members. "In order to have a society in which public issues can be openly and vigorously debated," he insisted, "it is not necessary to allow the brutalization of innocent victims."
SPEECH
With this blistering last line, Justice Alito ***rejected*** the majority's conception that for free speech to flourish, ***hateful speech*** must be allowed to exist.

After Charlottesville, it can be ***hard to accept*** the free speech principles that ***Snyder v. Phelps*** prescribes. Hate speech about matters of ***public concern,*** in ***public places,*** is entitled to full First Amendment protection. Just as with the Jehovah's Witnesses in ***Barnette,*** civil rights activists in ***Sullivan,*** Vietnam war protesters in ***Tinker*** and ***Cohen,*** and a pornographer in ***Hustler,*** the Supreme Court has resolved that ***controversial*** and ***objectionable speech*** should be ***safeguarded*** despite how much people may object to the content of that speech.
HUSTLER

At the same time, it is also important to recognize that the protection of ***hate speech*** as a matter of free speech law in no way ***obligates*** us as a society to accept the messages of hate or to turn a blind eye to the ***harm*** that such words can cause.

In addition, the ***Snyder*** case also reminds us that the government can impose ***time, place,*** and ***manner*** restrictions on demonstrations for a wide range of ***content-neutral*** reasons. For example, a city may constitutionally require protesters on two sides of an issue be ***separated*** for public safety (as long as neither side is privileged or disadvantaged because of their viewpoints), require the submission of pre-march plans, and set boundaries on the use of public property.

And, of course, violence of ***any kind,*** including the terrorist car-attack that took the life of ***Heather Heyer,*** can be prosecuted without any First Amendment restrictions. Case in point, the "avowed neo-Nazi" who killed Heyer was sentenced to life in prison for ***murder*** and ***federal hate crimes.***

This is the state of the law on hate speech today, and given the Supreme Court's relatively recent ***recommitment*** to these principles, by a broad coalition of liberal and conservative justices, it seems unlikely it will change anytime soon. Nevertheless, given the seeming ***resurgence*** of neo-Nazism in this country, this approach can be ***disturbing*** enough to shake the confidence of even the most ***stalwart*** First Amendment adherent.

Returning to the combatants in the ***Snyder*** case, we can see one justification for free speech including hate speech—the ability of raucous debate to ***change people's minds***—play out in very unexpected ways.

Megan Phelps-Roper, granddaughter of Westboro founder ***Fred Phelps,*** responded to the news of their Supreme Court victory in her ***typical*** fashion: She used social media to triumphantly proclaim their church's ***joy*** in the face of others' ***misery.***

DESTRUCTION
IS
IMMINENT
SUPREME
COURT

Megan had become her church's social media spokesperson, saying, "The Lord has given us a new platform." She described using "Twitter to ***bait celebrities*** with anti-gay messages, to ***publicly celebrate*** Japan's Fukushima nuclear disaster, and to debate the merits of the ***Snyder*** case with anyone who would listen."

And then, discussions she had with people on Twitter actually led her to begin ***questioning*** her faith. One turning point came when an Israeli Jewish blogger used New Testament quotations to dispute Westboro's belief in the ***death penalty*** for gay people. Megan began to consider "if the church was wrong" about these issues, "what ***else*** were we wrong about?"

As Megan put it, there were "these individuals who found ways of *kindly* and *effectively challenging* [her] beliefs at Westboro." Her hate speech had brought her in touch with *counterspeech.*
Eventually, in 2012, at the age of twenty-six, she *walked out* and left the Westboro Baptist Church. She had left most of her family, and their hateful beliefs, behind *for good.*

Now Megan uses her story to show that it is possible to break through the walls of our increasingly polarized society in which we frequently demonize the other side.

The good news is that it's *simple,* and the bad news is that it's *hard.* We have to *talk and listen to* people we *disagree with.*

From her personal experience, she sees the growing popularity of the idea that "refusing to grant mainstream *platforms* to *hated ideas* will halt their spread...[as] a fundamentally *flawed* strategy, one that ignores the practicalities of human nature."

"The principles enshrined in the First Amendment," says Megan, "are no less relevant to *social media* than they are in *public spaces:* that *open discourse* and dialectic is the most effective enabler of the *evolution* of individuals and societies."

Megan's transformation mirrors the change of heart experienced by **Albert Snyder.** After the ruling, which came the day before the **fifth anniversary** of Matthew's death, Snyder spoke out at a press conference: "We found out today that we can no longer bury our dead with dignity. [I'm] just very **disappointed** in America today."

Over time, Albert's feelings toward the Supreme Court and free speech **evolved.** By 2019, in an interview on the legal podcast *Unprecedented,* Albert expressed **different** feelings about the Supreme Court and free speech.

My son **fought** and **died** for **freedom of speech,** and I do understand what they did, and I may not have when the decision came down. I remember being **very upset,** but the reality set in, and I started to reflect on everything. And I realized that the Supreme Court made the **right decision,** as **painful** as it was.

With that simple statement of acceptance, two First Amendment foes had come to a profound agreement about the meaning of free speech in America. Sometimes the **theoretical power** of free speech can be realized even in the most **trying circumstances** of the **real world.**

Chapter 10: SOCIAL MEDIA, PUBLIC PARKS, AND THE "VAST DEMOCRATIC FORUMS of the INTERNET"

Sacha Baron Cohen, the comedian and actor famous for ***pranking*** people on camera as ***Borat*** and other fictional characters, walked into the ***Anti-Defamation League's*** 2019 summit, and it was ***no joke.***
In a scathing speech, he blamed ***surging hate crimes*** around the globe on "a handful of ***internet companies*** that amount to the ***greatest propaganda machine in history."***

Cohen warned that "our pluralistic democracies are on a precipice... and the role of social media could be determinant."

Pointing the finger at the group he dubbed the ***Silicon Six***—the billionaire leaders of ***Facebook, Google, YouTube,*** and ***Twitter***—he called for "a fundamental ***rethink*** of social media and how it spreads ***hate, conspiracies and lies."***

Last month, however, **Mark Zuckerberg** of Facebook delivered a **major speech** that, not surprisingly, warned against **new laws and regulations** on companies like his.
Law
Zuckerberg tried to portray this whole issue as "choices... around **free expression.**" That is ludicrous. This is not about limiting anyone's **free speech.**
This is about giving people, including some of the most **reprehensible people** on earth, the **biggest platform in history** to reach a third of the planet. Freedom of **speech** is not freedom of **reach.**

Cohen's keynote speech was just one of the more recent high-profile examples decrying the ***proliferation*** of hate speech online, and demanding that social media companies ***remove*** hate speech ***more aggressively*** from their platforms.

In ***Lindy West's*** feminist memoir *Shrill,* she describes being "on the receiving end of a viral internet ***hate mob,"*** including threats to ***rape*** and ***kill her,*** for having the temerity to suggest "that comedy might have a ***misogyny problem."***

shrill
lindy west

"It's hard to convey the confluence of galloping adrenaline and roaring dread," she wrote of the experience. "It is drowning and falling all at once."

After the release of the ***female-led*** remake of the *Ghostbusters* movie, costar and comedian ***Leslie Jones*** was subjected to hundreds of ***racist*** and ***sexist tweets.*** Jones took the unusual step of ***challenging*** and ***retweeting*** the horrid comments that she received, and the online abuse that she had been suffering received national news coverage.

ANSWER THE CALL
GHOSTBUSTERS
IN THEATERS
JULY 15

Twitter's *CEO*, ***Jack Dorsey,*** then reached out to Jones, and the company released a statement:

"We know many people believe we have not done enough to curb this type of behavior on Twitter.

"We agree."

If it takes a savvy ***movie star*** and a ***CEO*** to deal with such a high-profile onslaught of ***hate,*** what relief could Twitter's regular 300 million users hope for?

Hate speech and personal attacks by online trolls are of course just part of the problems plaguing social media. As the United Nations' special rapporteur on the promotion and protection of the right to freedom of opinion and expression has observed:

UNITED NATIONS

"Hatred is spreading through [online platforms] with the help of manufactured amplification; incitement to violence and discrimination seem to flow through their veins; and they have become highly successful and profitable zones for disinformation, election interference, and propaganda."

Given that ***seven in ten adults*** use social media, the scale and importance of these internet speech issues are undeniable.

FAKE NEWS

In our online lives today, ***burning questions*** about social media speech appear before us even faster than we can scroll through our feeds. Can hate speech on social media be ***restricted?*** What about the spread of ***"fake news"*** posts? Are government officials free to ***block users*** from their social media accounts?

Although social media hardly seems like ***cutting-edge technology*** anymore, the Supreme Court has only very recently even ***started*** to address "the relationship between the First Amendment and the modern Internet."

To comprehend how we can begin to approach free speech questions involving social media, we need to first ask how the First Amendment applies to ***restrictions*** on internet speech. For the Supreme Court, the answer would turn on how much cyberspace is like a ***public park IRL.****

On April 27, 2010, ***Lester Gerard Packingham*** was thrilled to have beaten a ***traffic ticket,*** and so he did what many of us do to share our good fortune: He went on ***Facebook.***

facebook.com

J.r. Gerrard

J.r. Gerrard Man God is Good! How about I got so much favor they dismissed the ticket before court even started? No fine, no court cost, no nothing spent...... Praise be to GOD, WOW! Thanks JESUS!

April 27 at 9:04am

Unfortunately for Packingham, around the same time, ***Officer Brian Schnee*** of the Durham Police Department was investigating ***registered sex offenders*** who were violating a North Carolina law that prohibited them from accessing ***social media.***

Officer Schnee saw the traffic ticket statement on Facebook, posted by someone named ***"J.R. Gerrard."*** Looking at the profile photo, Schnee thought he recognized the man as a ***sex offender.***

J.r. Gerrar
the ticket b
Praise be
April 27 at

*"IRL" is an acronym for "in real life," which is often used in social media communication to draw a contrast between real and online experiences.

So he tracked down the court records of ***traffic tickets*** dismissed around the time of the post, and came up with ***Packingham's*** name. Schnee followed up by obtaining a ***search warrant*** for Packingham's home, which turned up the ***evidence*** needed to confirm that Packingham had been using ***Facebook*** under the alias ***J.R. Gerrard.***

SEARCH WARRANT

A year later, Packingham was ***tried*** for violating North Carolina law, Section 14-202.5, which made it a ***crime*** for a registered sex offender "to access a ***commercial social networking Web site*** where the sex offender knows that the site permits ***minor children*** to become members or to create or maintain personal Web pages."

The ***purpose*** of the law was to prevent sex offenders from ***gathering information*** about children in order "to target an ***unwitting victim...*** under the guise of familiarity or shared interests." Since 2008 the law had applied to about ***20,000*** North Carolinians and more than 1,000 people had been prosecuted for violating it.

At trial, the basis for Packingham being on the sex offenders registry was presented to the ***jury.*** Nine years before, when Packingham was twenty-one years old, "he had sex with a 13-year-old girl," and pleaded guilty to "taking indecent liberties with a child."

Packingham was on ***supervised probation*** for ***two years,*** and had not had any problems with the law since his conviction. Prosecutors did not claim that he had contacted a minor or committed ***any other illegal acts*** on the internet.

PROBATION

Packingham was found ***guilty*** and sentenced to up to ***eight months of imprisonment,*** but any jail time was ***suspended*** and he was placed on supervised probation.

On appeal, the law was ***struck down*** for ***violating*** the ***First Amendment.*** The Court of Appeals for North Carolina held the law ***unnecessarily*** prevented "a wide range of ***communication*** and ***expressive activity*** unrelated to achieving" the state's legitimate interest in ***protecting children*** from sex offenders.

NORTH CARO
SECTION
OLINA LAW
14-202.5

The North Carolina Supreme Court ***disagreed*** and ruled, 4 to 2, that the law was "constitutional in all respects" and "carefully tailored."

NORTH CAROLINA LAW
SECTION 14-202.5

North Carolina's highest court also found that the law provided access to websites that served as sufficient ***alternatives*** to social media, giving the ***Paula Deen Network*** and a local ***NBC*** station as (particularly ***unconvincing)*** examples.

PDN
WRAL•com

When the Supreme Court granted review in Packingham v. North Carolina, it was not clear how eager the justices would be to directly engage with the social media aspects of the case. However, at oral argument in 2017, their questioning quickly made clear that the nature of social media was central to their views about speech limits.

Chief Justice John Roberts expressed dissatisfaction with the lack of ***precedent*** regarding the First Amendment and social media. "We don't have a lot of ***history*** here concerning access to websites and all the sort of things we're dealing with here," he said, referring in part to the "broad access to minors" that the internet provides.

Packingham's lawyer, ***David Goldberg,*** agreed that "as with any manner of new technologies the Court has confronted, there isn't...a framing... or reconstruction-era analogue."

However, he pointed out that "when you talk about all the things that the State historically has restricted, they never said you lose your right to publish a newspaper because you've been convicted" of a crime. Regardless of the technology, Goldberg contended, the wide-ranging post-prison speech restrictions of the North Carolina law was still historically ***unprecedented.***

JAIL

Expressing concern about "the safety of children," ***Justice Ruth Bader Ginsburg*** wanted to know: "Suppose the law simply said that someone who was a sex offender could not communicate with a minor on social media. Would you agree that that would be constitutional?" Goldberg initially ***hedged,*** but then agreed that "it probably ***would be.***"

Goldberg's reluctance seemed misplaced, as if he didn't recognize that accepting the limitation presented by Ginsburg would support his case. If there was a less speech-restrictive alternative available to North Carolina that still served the state's goal of protecting children, then the Court would likely find the current law to be overbroad and too restrictive.

Robert C. Montgomery, senior deputy attorney general of North Carolina, spoke for less than a minute before being interrupted by Justice Elena Kagan.

So a person in this situation, for example, cannot go onto the President's Twitter account to find out what the President is saying today? Not only the President. I mean, we're sort of aware of it because the President now uses Twitter. But in fact, everybody uses Twitter.
All 50 governors, all 100 senators, every member of the House has a Twitter account. So this has become...[a] crucially important channel of political communication. And a person couldn't go onto those sites and find out what these members of our government are thinking or saying or doing; is that right?

Montgomery had **no choice** but to answer, "That's right. However, there are alternatives. Usually those congressmen also have their own web page."
The unsatisfying quality of that alternative lingered only for a moment as **Justice Anthony Kennedy** built on Kagan's comments.
Well, it seems to me... assuming we had a **public square** a hundred years ago, could you say that this person couldn't go into the public square?...The sites that Justice Kagan has described and their utility...are **greater** than the communication you could [have] **ever had,** even in the paradigm of public square.
Justice Kennedy's focus here on **public squares** is referring to the idea that in public spaces (sometimes called **"public forums"** by the Court), where people can freely gather and talk, freedom of speech should receive the **highest level** of First Amendment protection.
In response, Montgomery accepted the metaphor but argued that "in essence, States have said that sex offenders can't go into the **public square;** that they can't go into **parks** or they...can't go near **playgrounds.**"

50 million Americans use [social media] for religious community purposes. So whether it's political community, whether it's *religious* community, I mean, these sites have become *embedded* in our culture as ways to *communicate* and ways to exercise our *constitutional rights,* haven't they?

Montgomery tried hard to maintain that "there are *other* alternatives, still. This is a *part* of the Internet, but it's not the *entire* Internet that is being taken away from these offenders. They can still have their *own blog.* They can *read blogs.* They can do *podcasts.* They can go to *nytimes.com.* They can do *other things* to communicate with people."

NYT

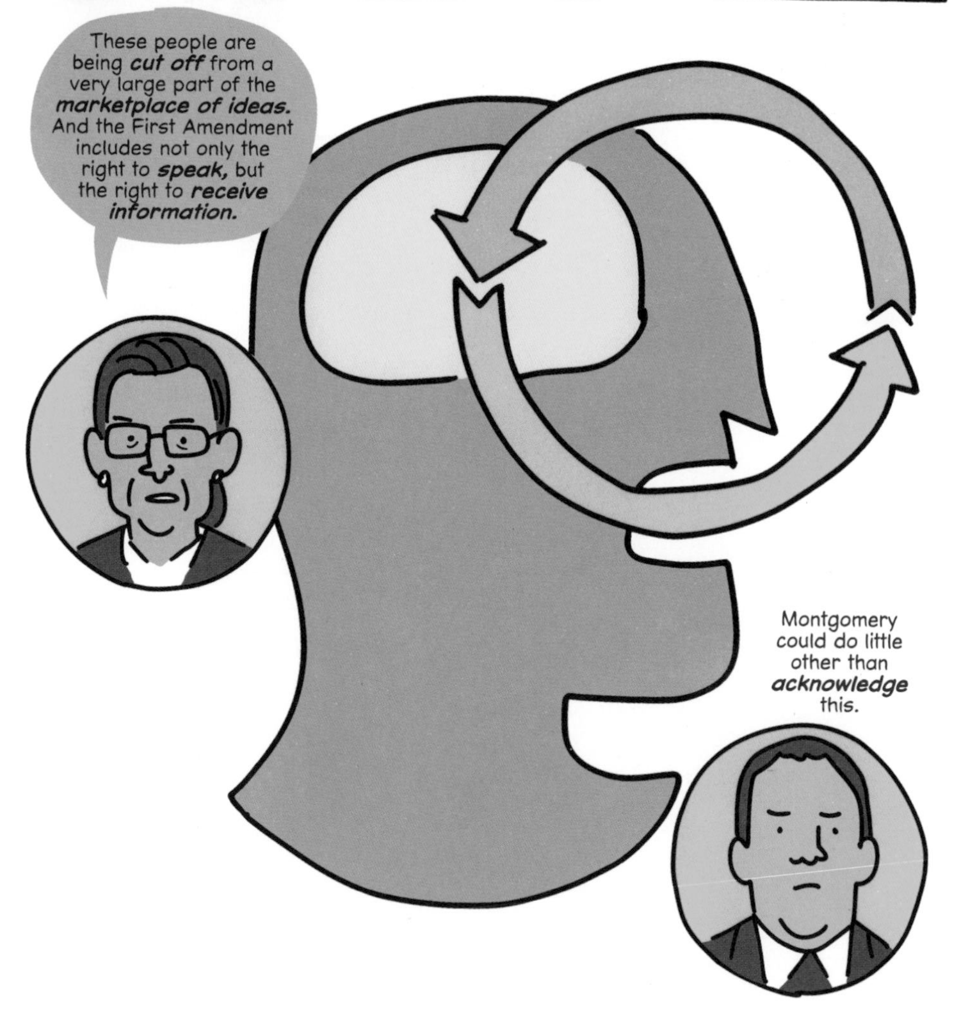
These people are being *cut off* from a very large part of the *marketplace of ideas.* And the First Amendment includes not only the right to *speak,* but the right to *receive information.*
Montgomery could do little other than *acknowledge* this.

Justice Samuel Alito challenged the idea of social media as *vital* to contemporary life, and pushed back during Goldberg's final minutes of rebuttal.
Now, I know there are people who think that life is *not possible* without Twitter and Facebook and these things and that 2003 was the *dark ages...*
He remarked somewhat sarcastically.
But if people got along perfectly well without social media such a relatively short time ago, and some people still do, then Alito wanted to know how taking away these new "channels of communication" could really be such a *dramatic limitation* on speech?
It is an extraordinary argument to say *not everybody* does it. I don't think that's the *test.* The test is how much of your core First Amendment activity is foreclosed.
And the ability to speak with this networked group of people all *over the world* is as strong—this is, as Justice Kennedy said, well *beyond* the traditional *town square.*

The vote in favor of Packingham was unanimous. Justice Kennedy wrote the opinion of the Court.
A fundamental principle of the First Amendment is that all persons have access to places where they can speak and listen, and then, after reflection, speak and listen once more. The Court has sought to protect the right to speak in this spatial context.
A basic rule, for example, is that a street or a park is a quintessential forum for the exercise of First Amendment rights. Even in the modern era, these places are still essential venues for public gatherings to celebrate some views, to protest others, or simply to learn and inquire.
While in the past there may have been difficulty in identifying the most important places (in a spatial sense) for the exchange of views, today the answer is clear. It is cyberspace—the vast democratic forums of the Internet in general, and social media in particular.

"While we now may be coming to the realization that the ***Cyber Age*** is a revolution of ***historic*** proportions, we cannot appreciate yet its full dimensions and vast potential to alter how we ***think, express ourselves,*** and ***define*** who we want to be."
"As a result, the Court must exercise ***extreme caution*** before suggesting that the First Amendment provides ***scant protection*** for access to vast networks in that medium."

Turning to evaluate the North Carolina statute, Kennedy recognized the ***significant interest*** of protecting "children and other victims of sexual assault from abuse." However, "the law must not burden ***substantially more speech*** than is ***necessary*** to further the government's legitimate interests."

Kennedy noted that states could constitutionally "enact ***specific,*** narrowly tailored laws that prohibit a sex offender from engaging in conduct that often presages a sexual crime, like ***contacting a minor*** or using a website to ***gather information*** about a minor."
Yet that was not what had occurred here. To the ***contrary,*** the Court found the statute at issue was "***unprecedented*** in the scope of First Amendment speech it burdens."

By prohibiting sex offenders from using those websites, North Carolina with one broad stroke ***bars access*** to what for many are the principal sources for ***knowing current events,*** checking ads for ***employment, speaking*** and ***listening*** in the ***modern public square,*** and otherwise exploring the ***vast realms*** of ***human thought*** and ***knowledge.***

These websites can provide perhaps the most ***powerful*** mechanisms available to a private citizen to make his or her voice heard. They allow a person with an Internet connection to become a ***town crier*** with a voice that resonates ***farther*** than it could from any soapbox.
In sum, to foreclose access to social media altogether is to prevent the user from engaging in the legitimate ***exercise*** of ***First Amendment rights.***
Therefore, the Court agreed that there was ***no choice*** but that the "law must be held invalid."
Still, there was ***disagreement*** as to the ***scope*** of the opinion. Justice Alito wrote a ***concurring opinion,*** joined by ***Chief Justice Roberts*** and ***Justice Thomas,*** that took Kennedy to task because they believed he had gone ***too far.***
Troubled by what he called "the implications of the Court's ***unnecessary rhetoric,"*** Alito scolded the other justices for being "unable to resist musings that seem to equate the ***entirety*** of the internet with ***public streets*** and ***parks."***
He feared that states would consequently be "largely ***powerless*** to restrict even the most dangerous sexual predators from visiting any internet sites, including, for example, ***teenage dating sites*** and sites designed to permit ***minors*** to discuss personal problems with their peers."

The Court is correct that we should be cautious in applying our free speech precedents to the internet. Cyberspace is different from the physical world... we should proceed circumspectly, taking one step at a time. It is regrettable that the Court has not heeded its own admonition of caution.

Unlike the other contemporary speech controversies that we have explored, in this area of social media, the Supreme Court has not yet provided answers to the questions many Americans have at the beginning of the 2020s.

Unfortunately, ***Packingham*** doesn't tell us what can be done to mitigate the problems created by social media ***trolls*** and ***hate mobs. Sacha Baron Cohen*** will continue to tear into ***Mark Zuckerberg,*** but the Court has remained silent on how to combat ***Nazi propaganda*** on Facebook. However, while ***Packingham*** doesn't contain easy answers, it does provide us with constructive ***guidance*** on how to approach these issues within a First Amendment framework.

Remember that all social media platforms are ***private entities*** and so do ***not*** have to abide by the First Amendment. They can ***abridge*** the freedom of speech all they want.

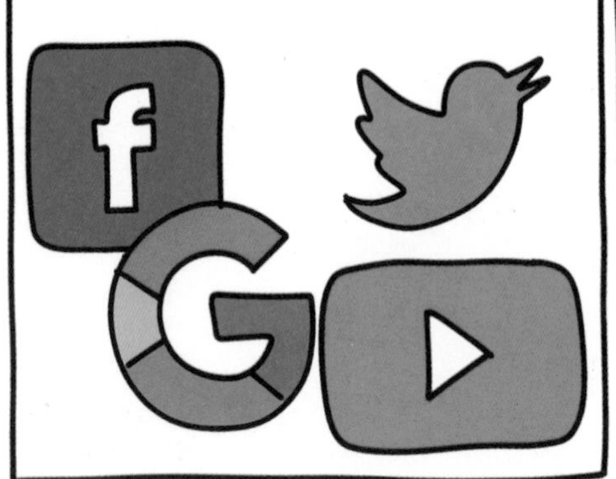

They can ***kick people off*** their platform, ***restrict*** speech based on its message, or ***refuse*** to accept ads from whomever they choose. These choices represent editorial decisions that reflect the ***free speech rights*** of the social media companies themselves.

While this raises a host of political and social issues (what if Twitter kicks off only right-wing conservatives, or Facebook restricts ***any*** post supporting Black Lives Matter?) the courts ***won't*** find these to be violations of the First Amendment.

Also, social media platforms are immune by federal statute for anything their users post, thanks to ***Section 230*** of the ***Communications Decency Act,*** enacted in 1996.

The ***Electronic Frontier Foundation,*** a leading digital rights advocacy organization, has described ***Section 230*** as "the most important law protecting internet speech," arguing that this relatively obscure provision has enabled "the kind of ***innovation*** that has allowed the Internet to thrive."

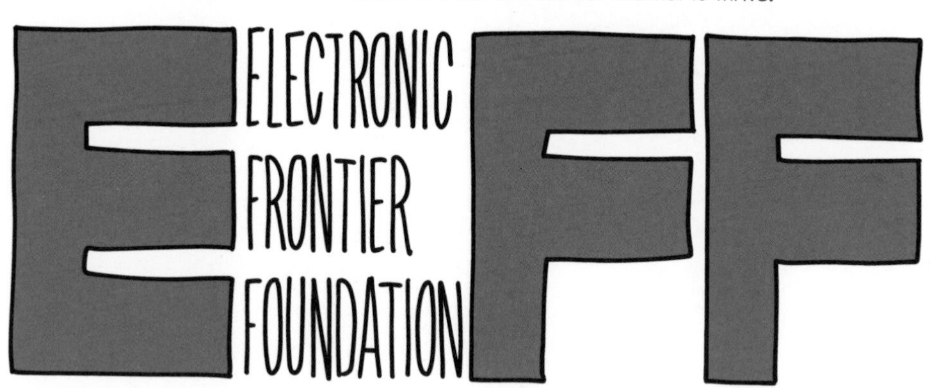
EFF
ELECTRONIC
FRONTIER
FOUNDATION

As a result, without foreseeable legal pressure from either ***lawsuits*** or ***constitutional challenges,*** any major social media reforms will most likely come from somewhere ***other*** than the courts.

Packingham at its core shows that all of the participating justices are ***unwilling*** to allow the government to place blanket restrictions on social media.

Packingham also highlights the threshold question of how should social media be treated: as *unexceptional,* and receive the *same* stringent defenses accorded to speech in general?
Or is social media so different that it should be treated as *exceptional,* a type of speech that can be more directly *regulated* in ways the press is *not?*
NEWS
Kennedy's opinion, with its embrace of past metaphors, sees social media as *unexceptional.*
Whereas Alito maintains that the internet is *exceptional* in ways that pose *greater dangers* and therefore may require *more intrusive* speech regulations.

Floyd Abrams, the country's preeminent First Amendment litigator, has spoken persuasively from an *unexceptionalist* perspective.

He says that we cannot deny that while the internet has created powerful new *town criers* (as Kennedy refers to them in *Packingham)* "those town criers now include *Nazis* and *child pornographers.*"

That does not mean that we should *change* our view of the First Amendment. None of the new technological innovations embedded [online] make anything *Justice Holmes* said any *less* true than when he said it.
[And] as the threats to Internet freedom mount—as they *will*—we should keep recalling that the only circumstances in which Holmes' (at least in his later *Abrams*-like) articulations would countenance *limitations* on speech is when an "immediate check is required to save the *country*," whenever crowded-theater speech would itself cause "immediate *panic*," or the like.
So as we go to sleep each night, we could do worse than to remind ourselves that "the ultimate good is better reached by the *free trade in ideas*" than any other way.
IDEAS!

This view ***may not*** suffice to make those of us worrying over the state of social media ***rest*** easy.

Yet, no matter how you look at contemporary social media challenges, it remains ***essential*** to understand the free speech rights that the Supreme Court has ***already established.***

The future of free speech is ***certainly online.*** How we as Americans seek to ***chart that future*** can only begin by taking in and ***learning*** from our First Amendment stories of the ***past.***

MY BODY MY
RISE UP

afterword

When new free speech questions arise in the future, taking stock of what First Amendment rights have already been established will always be a worthwhile starting point. In the preceding chapters, I recounted how ten of these rights have developed and continue to define American society today. My approach to telling these stories has been to focus on brevity and clarity as much as possible. To that end, and going even further, here is a list of the ten cases presented in this book distilled to their essence. As The Clash sing, "Know your rights, these are your rights. . ."

RIGHT TO ADVOCATE
FOR ILLEGAL ACTION
(UNLESS IT LIKELY CAUSES
IMMINENT HARM)

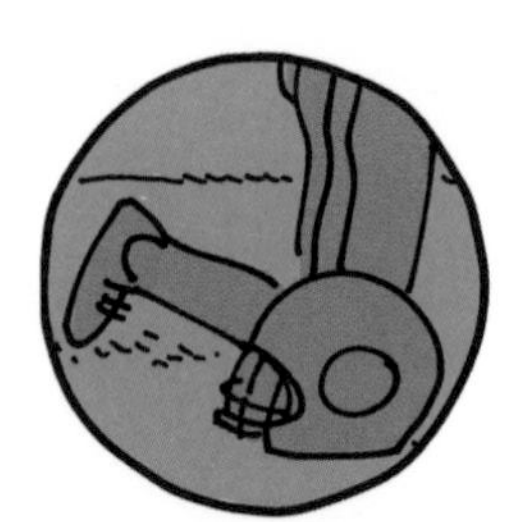

RIGHT NOT
TO SPEAK

The New York Tim

RIGHT TO CRITICIZE
PUBLIC FIGURES AND
MAKE MISTAKES

RIGHT TO
NONDISRUPTIVE
PROTEST IN SCHOOL

RIGHT TO OFFEND

NEWS

RIGHT TO
PUBLISH WITHOUT
BEING STOPPED

NO RIGHT TO
CURSE ON BROADCAST
TELEVISION AND RADIO

rry Falwell ta
about his first time.
You'll never forget yo

RIGHT TO PARODY

RIGHT TO
ESPOUSE THOUGHTS
PEOPLE HATE

RIGHT TO
USE SOCIAL MEDIA
AS A PUBLIC FORUM

I hope these bullet points will serve as helpful memory triggers when confronted with free speech challenges of all kinds.

And while knowing your rights is the best first step, applying those rights to uncharted contexts is a greater leap forward. Until now, this book has been more descriptive than prescriptive. But as advice for how to consider future free speech controversies, here are my recommended maxims, drawing on the principles behind these rights we have come to know well:

Protect Dissent

Defend the Press

Resist Government Speech Restrictions

Expand the Marketplace of Ideas

Allow Speakers to Express Messages How They Choose

Print them on a T-shirt, tape them up over your bed. Take them to heart, but not for granted. These lines don't encapsulate all the ideas behind our free speech rights today, but I believe they are uniquely beneficial for guiding us in the years to come.

We also may well need to put these precepts into practice sooner rather than later. Shortly after the end of World War II, George Orwell wrote a cautionary essay, observing:

> *The relative freedom which we enjoy depends on public opinion. The law is no protection. Governments make laws, but whether they are carried out, and how the police behave, depends on the general temper in the country. If large numbers of people are interested in freedom of speech, there will be freedom of speech, even if the law forbids it; if public opinion is sluggish, inconvenient minorities will be persecuted, even if laws exist to protect them.*

MY BODY MY
KEEP
OUR ARMS ARE TIRED FROM HOLDING THESE SIGNS SINCE THE 1920s
RISE UP
OUR RIGHTS ARE NOT UP FOR GRABS. NEITHER ARE WE.

Orwell's insights still feel essential and relevant today, as free speech values seem to be on the cusp of change, no matter how steadfast our First Amendment legal protections appear to be.

Having read this book, you can make a difference in shaping public opinion on free speech. You have the knowledge to speak freely with confidence. But even more importantly, you also have the power to engage in debate about legislation and policies that curtail speech or champion it. Although ultimately the Supreme Court will be the final word in determining First Amendment law, the process of getting reviewed by the highest court is long and unlikely. Meanwhile, speech happens on the ground every day—at schools, on community boards, in houses of worship, at city council meetings—and these local places are where an informed citizenry can have the greatest impact. Promoting and protecting free speech is not out of reach; it is an everyday, grassroots activity. Because the fight for free speech continues on, and now you can be a part of it too.

—Ian Rosenberg

UNITY
PEACE
EQUALITY
MY BODY
MY
THE FUTURE
IS
FEMALE
I AM NOT
UP FOR
LOVE

glossary of legal terms

Affirm: When an appellate court affirms a case, it agrees with the results reached by the court below and upholds the decision.

Bench Trial: A bench trial is one without a jury, in which the judge is the final decision maker.

Circuit Split: A circuit split occurs when at least two circuit courts in the U.S. Courts of Appeals rule differently on the same federal issue. Resolving a circuit split is often an important factor in the Supreme Court justices' decision to grant review of a case.

Compensatory and Punitive Damages: Compensatory damages, or "actual damages," are those awarded to a plaintiff for quantifiable injuries suffered, intended to restore the person financially to the place they were before the injury. Punitive damages are those awarded to punish the defendant for their intentional wrongdoing and to deter anyone from committing such wrongful action.

Free Speech Absolutist: A free speech absolutist is someone who believes in the theory, often championed by Justice Black, that the government should literally "make no law" that restricts free speech or free press rights.

Grievance: A grievance is an employee's formal complaint regarding an alleged violation of a union agreement, which provides a procedure for reviewing and resolving that complaint.

Injunction: An injunction is a court order to stop, or sometimes continue, a particular action.

Majority, Concurring, and Dissenting Opinions: A majority opinion is the decision of an appellate court joined by more than half the members of the court reviewing that case. A concurring opinion is written by one of the members of the court who agrees with the majority on the result of the decision, but wants to express a different reason for reaching that decision. A dissenting opinion is written by a member of the court that explicitly disagrees with both the result and the reasons of the majority opinion. A dissenting opinion is not binding precedent, but can be influential in future cases and draw public attention to the issues discussed.

Pro Bono: Pro bono, which comes from a Latin term that means "for the public good," describes the practice of lawyers representing a client free of charge.

Solicitor General: The solicitor general is the fourth-highest-ranking person in the U.S. attorney general's office, whose primary role is to argue on behalf of the United States government in cases before the Supreme Court.

Temporary Restraining Order: A temporary restraining order is a short-term order that is granted when the party seeking it successfully demonstrates that immediate and irreparable harm will occur if no action is taken by the court.

selected bibliography

For a more in-depth discussion by this author on all the topics in *Free Speech Handbook*, see Ian Rosenberg, *The Fight for Free Speech: Ten Cases That Define Our First Amendment Freedoms* (New York: NYU Press, 2021).

For audio recordings of Supreme Court oral arguments, clear case summaries, and links to the full texts of Supreme Court decisions, see Oyez, www.oyez.org (oral argument quotations in this book are taken from Oyez transcripts). Two additional accurate and free resources for legal information are the Cornell Law School Legal Information Institute, www.law.cornell.edu, and The First Amendment Encyclopedia, www.mtsu.edu/first-amendment/encyclopedia.

CHAPTER 1

Abrams v. United States, 250 U.S. 616 (1919)

Paul Avrich, *Anarchist Portraits* (Princeton, NJ: Princeton University Press, 1988)

Abe Bluestein, ed., *Fighters for Anarchism: Mollie Steimer & Senya Fleshin, a Memorial Volume* (Minneapolis: Libertarian Publications Group, 1983)

Ronald K. L. Collins and Sam Chaltain, *We Must Not Be Afraid to Be Free: Stories of Free Expression in America* (New York: Oxford University Press, 2011) (inspiring and captivating narrative nonfiction)

Emma Goldman, *Living My Life, Vol. II* (New York: Dover, 1970)

Thomas Healy, *The Great Dissent: How Oliver Wendell Holmes Changed His Mind—and Changed the History of Free Speech in America* (New York: Henry Holt, 2013) (gripping intellectual history of Holmes and why he dissented in *Abrams*)

Peter Irons, *A People's History of the Supreme Court* (New York: Penguin, 1999)

Charles R. Lawrence III, "If He Hollers Let Him Go: Regulating Racist Speech on Campus," 1990 *Duke Law Journal* 431 (1990) (a foundational article on critical race theory)

Catherine A. MacKinnon, "The First Amendment: An Equality Reading," in *The Free Speech Century*, edited by Lee C. Bollinger and Geoffrey R. Stone (New York: Oxford University Press, 2019)

Richard Polenberg, *Fighting Faiths: The Abrams Case, the Supreme Court, and Free Speech* (Ithaca, NY: Cornell University Press, 1987) (richly detailed historical study of the *Abrams* case)

Geoffrey R. Stone, *Perilous Times: Free Speech in Wartime* (New York: W. W. Norton & Company, 2004)

Trevor Timm, "It's Time to Stop Using the 'Fire in a Crowded Theater' Quote," *Atlantic*, November 2, 2012

CHAPTER 2

Minersville School District v. Gobitis, 310 U.S. 586 (1940)

West Virginia State Board of Education v. Barnette, 319 U.S 624 (1943)

Kareem Abdul-Jabbar, "Why the NFL Player Protests Still Matter," *Guardian*, February 3, 2018

Michael Bennett and Dave Zirin, *Things That Make White People Uncomfortable* (Chicago: Haymarket Books, 2019)

Chris Biderman, "Transcript: Colin Kaepernick Addresses Sitting during National Anthem," Niners Wire, August 28, 2016, www.ninerswire.usatoday.com

Vincent Blasi and Seana V. Shiffrin, "The Story of *West Virginia State Board of Education v. Barnette*: The Pledge of Allegiance and the Freedom of Thought," in *First Amendment Stories*, edited by Richard W. Garnett and Andrew Koppelman (New York: Foundation Press, 2012)

Winston Bowman, "The Flag Salute Cases," Federal Judicial Center, 2017, www.fjc.gov

Nate Boyer, "An Open Letter to Colin Kaepernick, from a Green Beret-Turned-Long Snapper," *Army Times*, August 30, 2016

John Branch, "The Awakening of Colin Kaepernick," *New York Times*, September 7, 2017

Howard Bryant, *The Heritage: Black Athletes, a Divided America, and the Politics of Patriotism* (Boston: Beacon Press, 2018) (brilliant and insightful analysis of race, sports, and protest)

Howard Bryant, "Why It Matters That Roger Goodell Didn't Say Colin Kaepernick's Name," ESPN.com, June 6, 2020

Jennifer Lee Chan, "Colin Kaepernick Did Not Stand during the National Anthem," Niners Nation, August 27, 2016, www.ninersnation.com

Ta-Nehisi Coates, "Civil-Rights Protests Have Never Been Popular," *Atlantic*, October 3, 2017

Ronald K. L. Collins, "Thoughts on Hayden C. Covington and the Paucity of Litigation Scholarship," 13 *FIU Law Review* 599 (2019)

Justin Driver, *The Schoolhouse Gate: Public Education, the Supreme Court, and the Battle for the American Mind* (New York: Pantheon, 2018)

Richard J. Ellis, *To the Flag: The Unlikely History of the Pledge of Allegiance* (Lawrence: University Press of Kansas, 2005)

Harry Enten, "The NFL Protests May Be Unpopular Now, but That Doesn't Mean They'll End That Way," FiveThirtyEight, September 25, 2017, www.fivethirtyeight.com

Peter Irons, *The Courage of Their Convictions* (New York: Free Press, 1988)

Elahe Izad, "Black Lives Matter and America's Long History of Resisting Civil Rights Protesters," *Washington Post*, April 19, 2016

Malcolm Jenkins (@MalcolmJenkins), "#TheFightContinues," Twitter, May 23, 2018, www.twitter.com

John Legend, "The NFL Protests Are Patriotic," Slate, September 24, 2017, www.slate.com

Richard Panchyk, *Our Supreme Court: A History with 14 Activities* (Chicago: Chicago Review Press, 2006)

Shawn Francis Peters, *Judging Jehovah's Witnesses: Religious Persecution and the Dawn of the Rights Revolution* (Lawrence: University Press of Kansas, 2000) (deeply researched and revealing history of Jehovah's Witnesses' interaction with constitutional law)

Gregory L. Peterson, E. Barrett Prettyman Jr., Shawn Francis Peters, Bennett Boskey, Gathie Barnett Edmonds, Marie Barnett Snodgrass, and John Q. Barrett, "Recollections of *West Virginia State Board of Education v. Barnette*," 81 *St. John's Law Review* 755 (2007)

Eric Reid, "Why Colin Kaepernick and I Decided to Take a Knee" (op-ed), *New York Times*, September 25, 2017

Mark Sandritter, "A Timeline of Colin Kaepernick's National Anthem Protest and the Athletes Who Joined Him," SB Nation, September 25, 2017, www.sbnation.com

Steven H. Shiffrin, *The First Amendment, Democracy, and Romance* (Princeton, NJ: Princeton University Press, 1990) (argues that dissenters should be the central figures of First Amendment theory)

Leonard A. Stevens, *Salute! The Case of the Bible vs. the Flag* (New York: Coward, McCann & Geoghegan, 1973)

Steve Wyche, "Colin Kaepernick Explains Why He Sat during National Anthem," NFL.com, August 27, 2016, www.nfl.com

CHAPTER 3

New York Times Company v. Sullivan, 376 U.S. 254 (1964)

Taylor Branch, *Parting the Waters: America in the King Years 1954–63* (New York: Simon & Schuster, 1988)

Taylor Branch, *Pillar of Fire: America in the King Years, 1963–65* (New York: Simon & Schuster, 1998)

Andrew Cohen, "Today Is the 50th Anniversary of the (Re-)Birth of the First Amendment," *Atlantic*, March 9, 2014

Garrett Epps, "The Civil Rights Heroes the Court Ignored in *New York Times v. Sullivan*: Celebrations of This Landmark Case Are Incomplete Without Any Mention of Ralph David Abernathy, S. S. Seay Sr., Fred L. Shuttlesworth, and J. E. Lowery," *Atlantic*, March 20, 2014

David J. Garrow, *Bearing the Cross: Martin Luther King, Jr., and the Southern Christian Leadership Conference* (New York: HarperCollins, 1986)

Fred Gray, *Bus Ride to Justice: Changing the System by the System—the Life and Works of Fred Gray* (Montgomery, AL: NewSouth Books, 2013)

Fred D. Gray, "The Sullivan Case: A Direct Product of the Civil Rights Movement," 42 *Case Western Reserve Law Review* 1223 (1992)

Kermit L. Hall and Melvin I. Urofsky, *New York Times v. Sullivan: Civil Rights, Libel Law and the Free Press* (Lawrence: University Press of Kansas, 2011)

Elena Kagan, "A Libel Story: Sullivan Then and Now (reviewing Anthony Lewis, *Make No Law: The Sullivan Case and the First Amendment* (1991))," 18 *Law and Social Inquiry* 197 (1993).

Harry Kalven Jr., "The New York Times Case: A Note on 'The Central Meaning of the First Amendment,'" 1964 *Supreme Court Review* 191 (1964)

Lee Levine and Stephen Wermiel, *The Progeny: Justice William J. Brennan's Fight to Preserve the Legacy of* New York Times v. Sullivan (Chicago: ABA Publishing, 2014)

Anthony Lewis, *Make No Law: The Sullivan Case and the First Amendment* (New York: Vintage Books, 1991) (the classic telling of the *Sullivan* story and its impact)

Catherine A. MacKinnon, "The First Amendment: An Equality Reading," in *The Free Speech Century*, edited by Lee C. Bollinger and Geoffrey R. Stone (New York: Oxford University Press, 2019)

Thurgood Marshall, "Commentary: Reflections on the Bicentennial of the United States Constitution," 26 *Valparaiso University Law Review* 21 (1991)

National Archives, "Advertisement, 'Heed Their Rising Voices,' *The New York Times*, March 29, 1960," www.archives.gov

Richard Panchyk, *Our Supreme Court: A History with 14 Activities* (Chicago: Chicago Review Press, 2007)

Mary-Rose Papandrea, "The Story of *New York Times Co. v. Sullivan*," in *First Amendment Stories*, edited by Richard W. Garnett and Andrew Koppelman (New York: Foundation Press, 2012)

Carlo A. Pedrioli, "*New York Times v. Sullivan* and the Rhetorics of Race: A Look at the Briefs, Oral Arguments, and Opinions," 7 *Georgetown Journal of Law & Modern Critical Race Perspectives* 109 (2015)

Gene Roberts and Hank Klibanoff, *The Race Beat: The Press, the Civil Rights Struggle, and the Awakening of a Nation* (New York: Random House, 2006)

Harrison E. Salisbury, *Without Fear or Favor: An Uncompromising Look at the* New York Times (New York: Times Books, 1980)

Stanford University's Martin Luther King, Jr. Papers Project, The Martin Luther King, Jr. Research and Education Institute, kinginstitute.stanford.edu

CHAPTER 4

Tinker v. Des Moines Independent Community School District, 393 U.S. 503 (1969)

Justin Driver, *The Schoolhouse Gate: Public Education, the Supreme Court, and the Battle for the American Mind* (New York: Pantheon Books, 2018) (a masterfully comprehensive analysis of constitutional issues in public education)

Vera Eidelman, "Can Schools Discipline Students for Protesting?" ACLU, February 22, 2018, www.aclu.org

Abe Fortas, *Concerning Dissent and Civil Disobedience* (New York: Signet Books, 1968)

Susan Dudley Gold, *Tinker v. Des Moines: Free Speech for Students* (Tarrytown, NY: Marshall Cavendish Benchmark, 2007) (excellent, concise overview of *Tinker* for young adults)

David Hogg and Lauren Hogg, *#NeverAgain: A New Generation Draws the Line* (New York: Random House, 2018)

David L. Hudson Jr., *Let the Students Speak!: A History of the Fight for Free Expression in American Schools* (Boston: Beacon Press, 2011)

John W. Johnson, *The Struggle for Student Rights:* Tinker v. Des Moines *and the 1960s* (Lawrence: University Press of Kansas, 1997) (thorough and essential review of the *Tinker* case and its participants)

Randall Kennedy, "The Forgotten Origins of the Constitution on Campus," *American Prospect*, December 28, 2017

Dahlia Lithwick, *Amicus with Dahlia Lithwick*, "Back to School Protest Special" (podcast), Slate, September 1, 2018, www.slate.com (interview with Mary Beth Tinker)

Dahlia Lithwick, "They Were Trained for This Moment: How

the Student Activists of Marjory Stoneman Douglas High Demonstrate the Power of a Comprehensive Education," Slate, February 28, 2018, www.slate.com

The March for Our Lives Founders, *Glimmer of Hope: How Tragedy Sparked a Movement* (New York: Penguin Random House, 2018)

Nico Perrino, *So to Speak: The Free Speech Podcast*, "From Black Armbands to the U.S. Supreme Court," January 10, 2019, www.sotospeak.libsyn.com (interview with Mary Beth Tinker and Robert Corn-Revere)

Catherine J. Ross, *Lessons in Censorship: How Schools and Courts Subvert Students' First Amendment Rights* (Cambridge, MA: Harvard University Press, 2015)

Mackenzie Ryan, "Tinker: School Walkouts Mark 'Turning Point' for Gun Violence, Teen Activism," *Des Moines Register*, March 14, 2018

Kathryn Schumaker, *Troublemakers: Students' Rights and Racial Justice in the Long 1960s* (New York: New York University Press, 2019)

Mary Beth Tinker, "'I'm Going to *Kill* You!,'" in *The Courage of Their Convictions*, edited by Peter Irons (New York: Free Press, 1988)

Tinker Tour USA, www.tinkertourusa.org (Mary Beth Tinker's website, "Empowering Youth Voices Through First-Amendment Activism")

Women's March Youth Empower, "Enough: National School Walkout," www.actionnetwork.org (organizers of the mass protest)

Vivian Yee and Alan Blinder, "National School Walkout: Thousands Protest against Gun Violence across the U.S.," *New York Times*, March 14, 2018

CHAPTER 5

New York Times Company v. United States, 403 U.S. 713 (1971)

Floyd Abrams, *Friend of the Court: On the Front Lines with the First Amendment* (New Haven, CT: Yale University Press, 2013)

Floyd Abrams, *Speaking Freely: Trials of the First Amendment* (New York: Viking, 2005) (the legendary First Amendment lawyer's remarkable memoir)

Michael Avenatti (@MichaelAvenatti), Twitter, March 8, 2018, www.twitter.com

Judith Ehrlich and Rick Goldsmith, dirs., *The Most Dangerous Man in America: Daniel Ellsberg and the Pentagon Papers* (ITVS/POV, 2009)

Daniel Ellsberg, *Secrets: A Memoir of Vietnam and the Pentagon Papers* (New York: Penguin, 2002)

Chris Geidner, "Trump Lawyers Are Considering a Challenge to Stop '60 Minutes' from Airing a Stormy Daniels Interview," Buzzfeed, March 11, 2018, www.buzzfeednews.com

National Archives, "Pentagon Papers," www.archives.gov

Presidential Recordings Digital Edition (Nixon Telephone Tapes 1971, edited by Ken Hughes) (Charlottesville: University of Virginia Press, 2014), www.prde.upress.virginia.edu

Michael Rothfeld and Joe Palazzolo, "Trump Lawyer Arranged $130,000 Payment for Adult-Film Star's Silence," *Wall Street Journal*, January 12, 2018

Scott Roxborough, "CBS News President David Rhodes on Stormy Daniels' '60 Minutes' Interview," *Hollywood Reporter*, March 13, 2018

David Rudenstine, *The Day the Presses Stopped* (Berkeley: University of California Press, 1996)

Neil Sheehan, "Vietnam Archive: Pentagon Study Traces 3 Decades of Growing U.S. Involvement," *New York Times*, June 13, 1971

"Text of Gurfein Opinion Upholding the Times and Kaufman Order Extending Ban," *New York Times*, June 20, 1971

Bob Woodward and Scott Armstrong, *The Brethren: Inside the Supreme Court* (New York: Simon & Schuster, 1979)

CHAPTER 6

Cohen v. California, 403 U.S. 15 (1971)

Susan J. Balter-Reitz, "*Cohen v. California*," in *Free Speech on Trial: Communication Perspectives on Landmark Supreme Court Decisions*, edited by Richard A. Parker (Tuscaloosa: University of Alabama Press, 2003)

Stephen Colbert, *Late Show with Stephen Colbert*, "Hire the Woman Who Was Fired for Flipping Off Trump," CBS, November 6, 2017, www.cbs.com

Petula Dvorak, "She Flipped Off President Trump—and Got Fired from Her Government Contracting Job," *Washington Post*, November 6, 2017

Daniel A. Farber, "Civilizing Public Discourse: An Essay on Professor Bickel, Justice Harlan, and the Enduring Significance of *Cohen v. California*," *Duke Law Journal* 283, 286 (1980)

Christopher M. Fairman, *FUCK: Word Taboo and Protecting Our First Amendment Liberties* (Naperville, IL: Sphinx Publishing, 2009)

Steve Herman (@W7VOA), Twitter, October 28, 2017, www.twitter.com

David L. Hudson Jr., "Paul Robert Cohen and 'His' Famous

Free-Speech Case," Freedom Forum Institute, May 4, 2016, www.freedomforuminstitute.org

Thomas G. Krattenmaker, "Looking Back at *Cohen v. California*: A 40 Year Retrospective from Inside the Court," 20 *William & Mary Bill of Rights Journal* 651 (2012)

Nadine Strossen, "Justice Harlan's Enduring Importance for Current Civil Liberties Issues, from Marriage Equality to Dragnet NSA Surveillance," 61 *New York Law School Law Review* 331 (2016–2017)

Bob Woodward and Scott Armstrong, *The Brethren: Inside the Supreme Court* (New York: Simon & Schuster, 1979)

CHAPTER 7

FCC v. Pacifica Foundation, 438 U.S. 726 (1978)

Samantha Bee, *Full Frontal with Samantha Bee* (TBS), "A Message from Sam," YouTube, June 6, 2018, www.youtube.com

George Carlin with Tony Hendra, *Last Words* (New York: Simon & Schuster, 2009)

George Carlin—Topic, "Seven Words You Can Never Say on Television," YouTube, April 29, 2016, www.youtube.com (full audio of the recording)

George Carlin—Topic, "Filthy Words," YouTube, April 29, 2016, www. youtube.com (full audio of the recording)

FCC, "Obscene, Indecent and Profane Broadcasts," September 13, 2017, www.FCC.gov

Melissa Mohr, *Holy Sh*t: A Brief History of Swearing* (New York: Oxford University Press, 2013) (a fascinating historical exploration of the origins and meaning of swearing)

Ivanka Trump (@IvankaTrump), Twitter, May 27, 2018, www.twitter.com

Adam M. Samaha, "Story of *FCC v. Pacifica Foundation*," in *First Amendment Stories*, edited by Richard W. Garnett and Andrew Koppelman (New York: Foundation Press, 2012)

James Sullivan, *Seven Dirty Words: The Life and Crimes of George Carlin* (New York: Da Capo Press, 2010)

Megh Wright, "Samantha Bee to Ivanka Trump: 'Do Something about Your Dad's Immigration Practices, You Feckless C*nt!,'" Vulture, May 31, 2018, www.vulture.com (video clip included at link, with Bee's unbleeped use of the word).

CHAPTER 8

Hustler Magazine, Inc. v. Falwell, 485 U.S. (1988)

Clay Calvert and Robert D. Richards, "Alan Isaacman and the First Amendment: A Candid Interview with Larry Flynt's Attorney," 19 *Cardozo Arts & Entertainment Law Journal* 313 (2001)

Jerry Falwell, *Strength for the Journey* (New York: Simon & Schuster, 1987)

Frances FitzGerald, "A Disciplined, Charging Army," *New Yorker*, May 18, 1981

Larry Flynt, "Larry Flynt: My Friend, Jerry Falwell," *Los Angeles Times*, May 20, 2007

Larry Flynt, *An Unseemly Man: My Life as Pornographer, Pundit, and Social Outcast* (Los Angeles: Dove Books, 1996)

Milos Forman, dir., *The People vs. Larry Flynt* (Columbia Pictures, 1996)

William T. Horner and M. Heather Carver, *Saturday Night Live and the 1976 Presidential Election* (Jefferson, NC: McFarland & Company, 2018)

Mike Hudson, "Falwell vs. Flynt," *Roanoke Times*, January 8, 1999

Lee Levine and Stephen Wermiel, *The Progeny: Justice William J. Brennan's Fight to Preserve the Legacy of* New York Times v. Sullivan (Chicago: ABA Publishing, 2014)

Joseph Russomanno, *Speaking Our Minds: Conversations with the People Behind Landmark First Amendment Cases* (Mahwah, NJ: Lawrence Erlbaum Associates, 2002)

Saturday Night Live (NBC), "Trump Press Conference Cold Open—SNL," YouTube, February 16, 2019, www.youtube.com (sketch that triggered Trump's call for "retribution")

Saturday Night Live (NBC), "White House Tree Trimming Cold Open—SNL," YouTube, December 16, 2017, www.youtube.com (sketch that triggered Trump's call for *SNL* to be "tested in courts")

Rodney A. Smolla, *Jerry Falwell v. Larry Flynt: The First Amendment on Trial* (New York: St. Martin's Press, 1988) (colorful and layered scrutiny of the legal battle between Falwell and Flynt)

Gloria Steinem, "Hollywood Cleans Up *Hustler*" (op-ed), *New York Times*, January 7, 1997

CHAPTER 9

Snyder v. Phelps, 562 U.S. 443 (2011)

Aaron Blake, "Trump Tries to Re-Write His Own History on Charlottesville and 'Both Sides,'" *Washington Post*, April 26, 2019

Adrian Chen, "Unfollow: How a Prized Daughter of the Westboro Baptist Church Came to Question Its Beliefs," *New Yorker*, November 23, 2015

Henry Louis Gates Jr., "War of Words: Critical Race Theory and the First Amendment," in *Speaking of Race, Speaking of Sex: Hate Speech, Civil Rights, and Civil Liberties*, edited by Henry Louis Gates Jr., Anthony P. Griffin, Donald E. Lively, Robert C. Post, William B. Rubenstein, and Nadine Strossen (New York: New York University Press, 1994)

Timothy J. Heaphy, "Final Report: Independent Review of the 2017 Protest Events in Charlottesville, Virginia," November 24, 2017, www.charlottesvilleindependentreview.com (the City of Charlottesville commissioned this report to provide "an independent evaluation of the City's handling of the summer protest events")

Mari J. Matsuda, Charles R. Lawrence III, Richard Delgado, and Kimberlé Williams Crenshaw, *Words That Wound: Critical Race Theory, Assaultive Speech, and the First Amendment* (Boulder, CO: Westview Press, 1993) (a seminal book with groundbreaking essays on critical race theory and the impacts of racist speech)

Megan Phelps-Roper, "I Grew Up in the Westboro Baptist Church. Here's Why I Left" (video), TED, February, 2017, ed.ted.com

Megan Phelps-Roper, *Unfollow: A Memoir of Loving and Leaving the Westboro Baptist Church* (New York: Farrar, Straus and Giroux, 2019)

Megan Phelps-Roper and Brittan Heller, "Conversion via Twitter" (video), Berkman Klein Center for Internet & Society at Harvard University, October 22, 2019, www.cyber.harvard.edu

Matthew S. Schwartz and Michael Vuolo, *Unprecedented*, "Middle Finger to God" (podcast), WAMU, November 13, 2019, www.wamu.org (engaging First Amendment podcast featuring interviews with Albert Snyder and Margie Phelps)

Steven H. Shiffrin, *What's Wrong with the First Amendment* (Cambridge, UK: Cambridge University Press, 2016)

Michael Signer, *Cry Havoc: Charlottesville and American Democracy*

Under Siege (New York: PublicAffairs, 2020) (former Charlottesville mayor's thoughtful and candid examination of the events leading up to the Unite the Right rally, the crisis and its aftermath)

Ellie Silverman, "From Wary Observer to Justice Warrior: How Heather Heyer's Death Gave Her Mom a Voice," *Washington Post*, February 1, 2018

Michael Smerconish, "He Looked Hate in the Eye," Politico, March 7, 2014, www.politico.com

Nadine Strossen, *Hate: Why We Should Resist It with Free Speech, Not Censorship* (New York: Oxford University Press, 2018) (definitive contemporary analysis of the reasons to support the Supreme Court's current approach on hate speech)

CHAPTER 10

Packingham v. North Carolina, 137 S. Ct. 1730 (2017)

Floyd Abrams, "On Thinking about the First Amendment and the Internet," in *Friend of the Court: On the Front Lines with the First Amendment* (New Haven, CT: Yale University Press, 2013) (I am pleased to note that I contributed research assistance to Abrams, as an associate at Cahill Gordon & Reindel, for the speech that was the basis for this chapter.)

Sacha Baron Cohen, "Keynote Address at ADL's 2019 Never Is Now Summit on Anti-Semitism and Hate: Remarks by Recipient of ADL's International Leadership Award," ADL, November 21, 2019, www.adl.org

Electronic Frontier Foundation, "Section 230 of the Communications Decency Act," www.eff.org

David Kaye, *Speech Police: The Global Struggle to Govern the Internet* (New York: Columbia Global Reports, 2019)

Andrew Liptak, "Leslie Jones: 'Hate Speech and Freedom of Speech Are Two Different Things,'" Verge, July 22, 2016, www.theverge.com

David Post, "Supreme Court Unanimously Overturns North Carolina's Ban on Social-Media Use by Sex Offenders," *Washington Post*, July 3, 2017

Mark Tushnet, "Internet Exceptionalism: An Overview from General Constitutional Law," 56 *William & Mary Law Review* 1637 (2015)

Lindy West, *Shrill: Notes from a Loud Woman* (New York: Hachette Books, 2016) (from the chapter "It's about Free Speech, It's Not about Hating Women")

afterword

George Orwell, "Freedom of the Park," *Tribune*, December 7, 1945 (accessible at www.orwellfoundation.com)

acknowledgments

My first thank you must be to my agent Carrie Hannigan, who had the crazy and amazing idea that my book on free speech could work as a graphic novel, and to pitch it to First Second. Thank you, Jesseca Salky, my agent and lawyer, for then making that opportunity successfully happen. Thank you, Nicola Wheir, my book coach extraordinaire, for all of your expert advice, which made this text better at every turn.

Thank you, Mark Siegel, for your vision, inviting me to be on your awesome World Citizen Comics team, and knowing that Mike Cavallaro would be a perfect partner for this adventure. Thank you to everyone at First Second, and particularly Kirk Benshoff, Robyn Chapman, MK Reed, and S. I. Rosenbaum for your collaborative spirit and support.

Thank you, Mike Cavallaro. This dream project would not have happened if not for you. Your visual genius, wit, and storytelling skills are second to none. You made these tales come alive, and even managed to make First Amendment law look fun and exciting, without losing any of the legal nuances that matter. Working with you has been a truly fulfilling creative experience, for which I am so grateful.

Thank you to my parents, Richard and Susan Rosenberg, for your love and for indulging my love of comics at an early age. Thank you to my wife, Caroline Laskow, who makes everything good in my life possible and whose creativity and dedication to making the world a better place (through free speech, protest, and acting local) continually inspires me. Finally, thank you to my children, Alice Lola Rosenberg and Leo Sidney Rosenberg, whose love of graphic novels and speaking freely is surpassed only by the love and happiness you give to our family. This book is dedicated to the two of you.

—Ian Rosenberg

Ian Rosenberg has more than twenty years of experience as a media lawyer and has worked as legal counsel for ABC News since 2003. A graduate of Cornell Law School, he is an Emmy-nominated documentary filmmaker and teaches media law at Brooklyn College. He is the author of *The Fight for Free Speech: Ten Cases That Define Our First Amendment Freedoms* (NYU Press).

Mike Cavallaro is from New Jersey and has worked in comics and animation since the early 1990s. His comics include Eisner Award–nominated *Parade (with Fireworks)*, *The Life and Times of Savior 28* (written by J. M. DeMatteis), *Foiled* and *Curses! Foiled Again* (written by Jane Yolen), *Decelerate Blue* (written by Adam Rapp), and the Nico Bravo series.